CAPSTONE REFERENCE

THE
ULTIMATE
STRATEGY
LIBRARY

THE 50 MOST INFLUENTIAL
STRATEGIC IDEAS OF ALL TIME

JOHN MIDDLETON

CAPSTONE

The right of John Middleton to be identified as the author of this book has been asserted in accordance with the Copyright, Designs and Patents Act 1988

First published 2003 by

Capstone Publishing Limited (a Wiley company)
8 Newtec Place
Magdalen Road
Oxford
OX4 1RE
United Kingdom
http://www.capstoneideas.com

CIP catalogue records for this book are available from the British Library and the US Library of Congress

ISBN 1-84112-180-0

Typeset in 10.5/13 pt Plantin
by Sparks Computer Solutions Ltd
http://www.sparks.co.uk
Printed and bound by
TJ International Ltd, Padstow, Cornwall

Substantial discounts on bulk quantities of Capstone Books are available to corporations, professional associations and other organizations. For details telephone Capstone Publishing on (+44-1865-798623), fax (+44-1865-240941) or email (info@wiley-capstone.co.uk).

CONTENTS

'To carve out a face in a mountain of stone
Day after day, one man alone
And it took twenty years just to get to his eyes
But he has found him a reason to rise.'

From the song 'Reason to Rise' by American singer-songwriter John Stewart

'Talk doesn't cook rice.'

Chinese proverb

ACKNOWLEDGEMENTS

I'd like to thank:

- John Moseley at Wiley, who showed that the skills of a top-class editor are like those of the very best waiters – hovering and helpful when needed, and nowhere to be seen when not.
- The 'Friends of Ultimate Strategy' – an unrivalled group of business brains whose advice, tips, and comments about which books should be featured here (and, just as crucially, which titles in their view didn't merit a place) helped me to end up with a final list that was a vast improvement over my initial attempt. The final decision though about what went in was mine, so I alone deserve it on the chin for any howlers, omissions, or glaring errors of judgement.
- All the writers and contributors to *Future Filter*, particularly Bob Gorzynski, whose regular pearls of wisdom have enhanced my understanding of business strategy.

Finally, for the seventh time, a huge thank you to Julie, Guy and Helena for allowing me the space to write this book, and giving me support and encouragement on the regular occasions I needed it. This book is dedicated to you three with all my love.

INTRODUCTION

In 1980, Michael Porter first published his seminal work *Competitive Strategy*, which rewrote the ground rules for all those looking at strategy. Two years later Tom Peters and Robert Waterman published *In Search of Excellence*, which quickly became an article of faith for managers around the globe.

Yet around twenty years later, despite the widespread use of universal tonics such as total quality management and business process re-engineering, strategy is still at the centre of management debate and we seem no closer to understanding what makes an organization successful. Richard Pascale, a leading management writer, puts it nicely: 'The sobering truth is that our theories, models, and conventional wisdom combined appear no better at predicting an organization's ability to sustain itself than if we were to rely on random chance'.

The Ultimate Strategy Library explores why strategy continues to excite, frustrate and intrigue us. It traces the history of strategic planning in business and looks at the major components of strategy in these early years of the twenty-first century. It examines the conventional strategic framework and asks how useful this paradigm has been in the past for understanding organizational success. Finally, it looks at current developments in strategic thinking, and at how things might evolve in the future.

At the heart of *The Ultimate Strategy Library* are reviews of 50 key books that explore various facets of strategy. The key ideas in each book are summarized and assessed.

For ease of reference, the books featured are presented in alphabetical order by author. In addition, there is an extensive annotated bibliography of another 50 books at the back of the book (also listed alphabetically by author), as well as a glossary of key strategy terms, and a guide to further sources of information for those wishing to delve deeper.

The unprecedented speed of change that confronts us, coupled with the rate at which our knowledge of what does and doesn't work in this new business environment is growing, has made the task of selecting the

Defining strategy

Scattered throughout this book, you will find a number of definitions of strategy offered by some of the finest thinkers in the field. You'll discover that there are many different perspectives on offer, with one unifying theme, namely that all definitions of strategy concern themselves with the future direction of the organization and the selection of a route map to guide the organization into that future. Strategy, then, is concerned with developing an understanding of the present situation ('where are we now'), the desired future position ('where do we want to be') and the path to take the organization from its present position into the future ('how do we get there').

This is not a simple three-step process. In my eyes, the strategic development process is not sequential. Rather it is iterative with the process of setting objectives, strategies and tactics deeply intertwined. It can be messy and experimental with critical information and resources flowing from the bottom up.

Hence my personal favourite definition: strategy is 'the management of ignorance'.

50 'best' books on strategy a tad daunting. All too often, books hailed on publication as ground-breaking have within a couple of years been fully absorbed into the strategic bloodstream, their once stunning insights reduced to the status of the blindingly obvious.

In selecting books for inclusion, I had two main aims: one was to represent the range of thinking that has emerged about strategy over the years (this quest for breadth rather than depth means that only one writer – Richard Pascale – has two books featured in the 50 chosen, whereas it would have been possible to fill the 50 places available with a handful of writers – Michael Porter, Henry Mintzberg and Peter Ducker, for example, have written well over that number of books between them!).

My second aim has been to pick out books in the main that have something practical to offer businesses over the next few years.

That said, there will inevitably be one or two books featured in *The Ultimate Strategy Library* whose impact will be short-lived. In recent times, this has been particularly evident with strategy books that have a strong technological focus. There have been some excellent books, but most have dated very rapidly.

It is equally inevitable that there will be new books appearing in the months and years ahead that would merit inclusion. These issues will be addressed by the publication, in due course, of a second edition.

It would be rash – and wrongheaded – to offer the titles featured in *The Ultimate Strategy Library* as a definitive overview of the field. In fact, I would welcome your suggestions for titles that you believe should have been included. In the meantime, here are 50 books whose common feature is that they all challenge our thinking about and inform our understanding of the strategic landscape.

John Middleton
john@thefridayfilter.com
Bristol, England
January 2003

A BRIEF HISTORY OF STRATEGY

Strategy has always been concerned with how to do things. Conventionally, strategy is taken to mean the game plan or road map of organizational change. Since strategy has its origins in military usage, we tend to think of it in terms of plans of attack or defence, competitive battlefields, and winners and losers. This is unfortunate, as strategy is as much to do with understanding the process of change as the tactics employed to deal with it. Moreover, strategy is more than a zero-sum game. It's not simply about competing for a bigger share of a finite market; it's about creating new markets to meet human needs in new and exciting ways. It's about creating the future. In the words of Gary Hamel and C K Prahalad in their book *Competing for the Future*: 'There is not one future but hundreds. There is no limit that says that most companies must be followers. Getting to the future first is not just about outrunning competitors bent on reaching the same prize. It is also about having one's own view of what the prize is. There can be as many prizes as runners; imagination is the only limiting factor.'

The military connotation is unfortunate in another, more obvious, way. Military strategy is the prerogative of generals; soldiers are expected to follow orders. While organizations frequently talk of empowerment and upward communication, when it comes to strategic decision-making, an essentially hierarchical mind-set often prevails. Sometimes, this is justified under the guise of the expertise required to understand the organization's 'complex' environment. Sometimes, it simply reflects the personal egos of key executives. Whatever the case, the message sent out to the organization is very damaging: 'we just don't trust you'.

Moving away from the military metaphor requires a fundamental shift in perspective; from the limited to the unlimited, from protective to creative, from sceptical to trusting, and from self-assurance to humility. It also requires seeing the part that all members of an organization play in challenging mind-sets, inventing new opportunities and creating the future. It means appreciating that every position in an organization, however 'humble', is absolutely vital in the making of strategy. It means recognizing the part that we all play in creating the future. Our best organizations can and do move away from the military metaphor.

The discipline of strategy has always incorporated new elements and strands. These strands are often interpreted as alternative ways of viewing strategy but in reality they can be seen as reflecting different aspects of the external environment and/or different time periods.

In the 1960s, for example, organizations faced a relatively stable environment with strong economic growth, which fostered a planning orientation.

One of the seminal influences on the development of thinking about strategy in the 1950s and 1960s was Pulitzer Prize-winning business historian Alfred D Chandler. His book *Strategy and Structure*, published in 1962, was characterized by an underlying assumption that organizations acted in a rational, sequential manner. In his book, Chandler defined strategy as 'the determination of the long-term goals and objectives of an enterprise, and the adoption of courses of action and the allocation of resources necessary for carrying out these goals'. Growth resulted from the awareness of the opportunities and needs to employ existing or expanding resources more profitably and efficiently. He saw structure as 'the design of the organization through which the enterprise is administered'. Chandler's famous conclusion, that structure follows strategy, was accepted as a fact of corporate life for decades until challenged in the 1980s and 1990s by the likes of Tom Peters and Richard Pascale.

In a similar vein, academic and consultant Igor Ansoff was in 1965 offering a highly prescriptive approach to strategy and advocating a heavy reliance on the use of analytical tools. Ansoff's particular contribution to the evolution of thinking about business strategy was to provide a rational model and a set of concepts and tools by which strategic and planning decisions could be made.

According to the Ansoff Model of Strategic Planning, the strategic decision-making process consists of what Ansoff called a 'cascade of decisions, starting with highly aggregated ones and proceeding toward the more specific'. Central to this concept was the notion of gap analysis. In fact, more specifically, Ansoff's whole approach revolved around the gathering of potentially vast quantities of data. As a result, many of his followers found themselves encountering a phenomenon which came to be known as 'paralysis by analysis'.

Through the 1960s and 1970s, then, there was an over-riding view in the business world that the future was readily predictable and business strategy was the means by which an organization's future could be pinpointed, planned for, and effectively managed.

Strategic planning began to be seen as a way of optimizing profit and growth in an organization. It was the recognition that many things had to be coordinated to be successful, especially in very large, complex companies, such as General Motors in the USA and Phillips in Europe. Strategy became a major role of senior management and acquired a collection of best practices and methods that became routine in all large companies. By the early 1970s, the largest corporations in the world had strategy departments. They varied in performance: some collected data about the industry the company was in and made suggestions, others thought about where a firm should go over many years, and yet others established planning techniques that were used at lower levels, for example, in divisions.

This world view was perpetuated by Michael Porter, arguably the most influential thinker and writer on strategic issues to have emerged in the last 25 years. When *Competitive Strategy* was published in 1980, Porter's generic strategies offered companies a rational and embraceable model for grasping and managing their future. According to Porter, a company finds itself in the midst of a set of competing forces that pit it not only against its direct competitors but also against its suppliers, customers, and those who may become its future competitors. Management's core challenge, he maintains, is to tighten the company's hold over its suppliers and customers and to find ways to keep both existing and future competitors at bay, protecting the firm's strategic advantages and allowing it to benefit maximally from them.

The essence of this theory is simple: the objective of a company is to capture as much as possible of the value that is embodied in its products and services. The problem is that there are others – customers, suppliers, and competitors among them – who want to do the same. As the economists point out, if there is genuine, free competition, companies can make no profits above the market value of their resources. The purpose of strategy, therefore, is to prevent such open and free competition: to claim the largest share of the pie while preventing others from eating your lunch, to mix metaphors.

The main problem with Porter's concept of companies, which has shaped the thinking of a generation of managers, is that it is based on a static view of the world, in which the size of the economic pie is given. In this zero-sum world, all that is left to be decided is how the pie is to be divided up, and corporate profits must indeed come at a cost to society.

Although Porter's take on strategy retains its adherents to this day, the 1990s saw a radical transformation of strategy away from its roots in long-term planning to a more holistic discipline concerned with aligning the organization to a rapidly changing world. Christopher A Bartlett and Sumantra Ghoshal captured this shift in a series of articles for the *Harvard Business Review* between November 1994 and May 1995. The authors explored a business environment in which over-capacity was the norm, markets were global, lines separating businesses were fuzzy, and, with equal access to technology, early-market entry advantages became minimal.

Bartlett and Ghoshal suggested that a change in management doctrine was needed to match this new landscape, namely that:

- Senior managers should change their own priorities and way of thinking. They should expand their focus from devising formal structures to developing organizational purpose.
- Companies should shift from top-down direction by managers who set the company vision and instead should encourage bottom-up initiatives from operating units, which are closest to customers.
- Top managers should shift from directing and correcting middle and frontline managers to creating an environment in which individuals monitor themselves.

In short, they argued that the traditional strategic paradigm, in which organizational structures and systems supported strategy, was being replaced by a more humanistic paradigm which relied more heavily on defining the purpose/vision of the organization and developing the skills to attain this vision.

Today, most strategic commentators maintain that a robust planning framework is still absolutely vital to the success of an organization, but that it is no longer sufficient by itself, given very rapid rates of change. Accordingly, in the early years of the twenty-first century, the emphasis has shifted to factors that allow organizations to develop adaptability and flexibility.

The Ultimate Strategy Library timeline

The pre-history of strategy

Sun Tzu *The Art of War* 500 BC
Nicoló Machiavelli *The Prince* 1513

1960–1979

Alfred Chandler *Strategy and Structure* 1962
Igor Ansoff *Corporate Strategy* 1965
Peter Drucker *The Age of Discontinuity* 1969

1980–1989

Michael Porter *Competitive Strategy* 1980
Alvin Toffler *The Third Wave* 1980
Richard Pascale and Anthony Athos *The Art of Japanese Management* 1981
Kenichi Ohmae *The Mind of the Strategist* 1982
Tom Peters and Robert Waterman *In Search of Excellence* 1982
Noel Tichy *Managing Strategic Change* 1983
Shoshana Zuboff *In the Age of the Smart Machine* 1988
Charles Handy *The Age of Unreason* 1989

1990–1994

Richard Pascale *Managing on the Edge* 1990
Peter Senge *The Fifth Discipline* 1990
Geoffrey Moore *Crossing the Chasm* 1991
Peter Schwartz *The Art of the Long View* 1991
Walt Wriston *Twilight of Sovereignty* 1992
Michael Hammer and James Champy *Reengineering the Corporation* 1993
John Kay *Foundations of Corporate Success* 1993
James Collins and Jerry Porras *Built to Last* 1994
Michael Goold, Andrew Campbell and Marcus Alexander *Corporate-Level Strategy* 1994

Gary Hamel and C K Prahalad *Competing for the Future* 1994
Henry Mintzberg *The Rise and Fall of Strategic Planning* 1994

1995–1999

Manuel Castells *The Information Age: Economy, Society and Culture* 1996/7/8
Andrew Grove *Only the Paranoid Survive* 1996
Frederick Reichheld *The Loyalty Effect* 1996
Robert S Kaplan and David P Norton *The Balanced Scorecard* 1996
— Frances Cairncross *The Death of Distance* 1997
Regis McKenna *Real Time* 1997
Arie de Geus *The Living Company* 1997
Thomas Stewart *Intellectual Capital* 1997
Watts Wacker and Jim Taylor *The 500 Year Delta* 1997
Shona Brown and Kathleen Eisenhardt *Competing on the Edge* 1998
— Stan Davis and Christopher Meyer *Blur* 1998
— Larry Downes and Chunka Mui *Unleashing the Killer App* 1998
Kevin Kelly *New Rules for the New Economy* 1998
— Carl Shapiro and Hal R Varian *Information Rules* 1999
Charles Ferguson *High Stakes, No Prisoners* 1999
Paul Hawken, Amory B Lovins and L Hunter Lovins *Natural Capitalism* 1999
Tom Petzinger *The New Pioneers* 1999
B Joseph Pine and James H Gilmore *The Experience Economy* 1999
David Siegel *Futurize Your Enterprise* 1999
Michael J Wolf *The Entertainment Economy* 1999

2000–

Robert Baldock *The Last Days of the Giants?* 2000
— Philip Evans and Thomas Wurster *Blown to Bits* 2000
Sumantra Ghoshal and Christopher A Bartlett *The Individualized Corporation* 2000
— Mary Modahl *Now or Never* 2000
Jonas Ridderstråle and Kjell Nordström *Funky Business* 2000
Don Tapscott *Digital Capital* 2000

The Ultimate Strategy Library: key themes

If you are interested in particular aspects of strategy, you might find the following sub-divisions helpful for accessing the most relevant reviews.

The origins of strategy

Igor Ansoff *Corporate Strategy*
Alfred Chandler *Strategy and Structure*
Nicoló Machiavelli *The Prince*
Sun Tzu *The Art of War*

The futurists

Peter Drucker *The Age of Discontinuity*
Alvin Toffler *The Third Wave*
Watts Wacker and Jim Taylor *The 500 Year Delta*

Strategy and technology

Frances Cairncross *The Death of Distance*
Manuel Castells *The Information Age: Economy, Society and Culture*
Stan Davis and Christopher Meyer *Blur*
Larry Downes and Chunka Mui *Unleashing the Killer App*
Philip Evans and Thomas Wurster *Blown to Bits*
Kevin Kelly *New Rules for the New Economy*
Mary Modahl *Now or Never*
Carl Shapiro and Hal R Varian *Information Rules*
David Siegel *Futurize Your Enterprise*
Walt Wriston *Twilight of Sovereignty*
Shoshana Zuboff *In the Age of the Smart Machine*

Strategy at the sharp end

Charles Ferguson *High Stakes, No Prisoners*
Andrew Grove *Only the Paranoid Survive*
Tom Petzinger *The New Pioneers*

All-time classics

Igor Ansoff *Corporate Strategy*
Gary Hamel and CK Prahalad *Competing for the Future*
John Kay *Foundations of Corporate Success*
Henry Mintzberg *The Rise and Fall of Strategic Planning*
Kenichi Ohmae *The Mind of the Strategist*
Richard Pascale and Anthony Athos *The Art of Japanese Management*
Richard Pascale *Managing on the Edge*
Michael Porter *Competitive Strategy*
Kenichi Ohmae *The Mind of the Strategist*

Strategic tools and models

Michael Goold, Andrew Campbell and Marcus Alexander *Corporate-Level Strategy*
Michael Hammer and James Champy *Reengineering the Corporation*
Robert S Kaplan and David P Norton *The Balanced Scorecard*
Geoffrey Moore *Crossing the Chasm*
Michael Porter *Competitive Strategy*
Peter Schwartz *The Art of the Long View*
Thomas Stewart *Intellectual Capital*
Noel Tichy *Managing Strategic Change*

Strategic philosophers

Charles Handy *The Age of Unreason*
Paul Hawken, Amory B Lovins and L Hunter Lovins *Natural Capitalism*
Kenichi Ohmae *The Mind of the Strategist*
Richard Pascale *Managing on the Edge*
Peter Senge *The Fifth Discipline*

The Ultimate
Strategy Library 50

IGOR ANSOFF

Corporate Strategy

1965

*C*orporate Strategy is one of the most important and influential books ever written on the subject. Its central idea is now accepted as conventional business wisdom, namely that managers should prepare for the future through systematic anticipation of future business challenges, and they should formulate appropriate strategic plans in response.

At the time of its publication, however, *Corporate Strategy* was breaking new ground. It was the first book to bring together a number of integrated strategic planning concepts that were 'invented' independently at various leading American companies, including the Lockheed Corporation, where Ansoff had worked in the 1950s and early 1960s. More significantly, the book presented several new theoretical concepts such as partial ignorance, business strategy, gap analysis, capability and competence profiles, synergy, and paralysis by analysis. In writing this book, Ansoff almost single-handedly created the vocabulary of modern-day strategy.

He also wrestled the topic away from the grip of the economists and number-crunchers. Before *Corporate Strategy* appeared, responsibility for strategic planning – insofar as it was acknowledged as a discipline at all – rested with the wrong people.

Ansoff was quite explicit about this. He wrote, 'Study of the firm has been the long-time concern of the economics profession: Unfortunately for our present purpose, the so-called micro-economic theory of the firm which occupies much of the economists' thought and attention, sheds relatively little light on decision making process in a real world firm.'

If Ansoff is not enamoured of economists, he is more at home with marketers. The so-called Ansoff Matrix is a well-known marketing tool that was first published in 1957 in the *Harvard Business Review*. Used by marketers who have aspirations of growth, it is a framework that helps businesses to characterize their strategic intentions. The Matrix offers four classifications:

- market penetration;
- product development;
- market development; and
- diversification.

Market penetration: existing markets/existing products

The 'steady as she goes' strategy implies the continuation of an existing strategy. This may be appropriate in the short term when the environment is stable or when the firm prefers to wait to see how situations develop before formulating a response. In the long term, these tactics are unlikely to be realistic or beneficial. In Ansoff's view, they may reflect a lack of strategic awareness on the part of the management team.

Product development: existing markets/new products

Product development involves the firm in substantial changes to its present product range, but it operates from the security of its established customer base. In R&D-intensive industries, product development may well be the main strategic thrust even though new product development is often risky and expensive.

Market development: new markets/existing products

Market development can include entering new geographical areas, promoting new uses for an existing product, and entering new market segments. It is an appropriate strategy to pursue when the organization's distinct competence rests with the product rather than the market.

Diversification: new markets/new products

Moving into a new market with a new product is an example of diversification, of which Ansoff identifies three types:

- *horizontal diversification* refers to the development of activities which are complementary to or competitive with the organization's existing activities;
- *vertical integration* refers to the development of activities which involve the preceding or succeeding stages in the organization's production process. Examples include the brewers' control of public houses, and the oil industry combining exploration, refining and distribution;
- *conglomerate diversification* refers to the situation where the new activity of the organization seems to bear little or no relation to its existing products or markets. An example would the Hanson Trust, with its interests in unconnected fields of engineering, batteries, building products and cigarettes.

Once an organization has clarity about its future intentions – whether to diversify, to take existing products/services into new markets, or whatever – the next step according to Ansoff is to conduct a Gap Analysis. This process has four steps:

- establish a set of objectives;
- estimate the difference or gap between the current position of the firm and the desired objective(s);
- identify one or more courses of action; and
- test these courses of action for their 'gap-reducing properties'. If the gap is substantially closed, Ansoff says that 'the course of action is accepted'; if not, try new alternatives.

In many ways, Ansoff was years ahead of his time. He was, for example, exploring the idea of 'competitive advantage' well before Michael Porter turned his mind to the topic in the 1980s. In other ways, Ansoff reveals his background as an engineer and a mathematician in his approach, and he has attracted criticism over the years for being too rational, prescriptive, and unwieldy. Ansoff, to his credit, was alert to these critical comments, even to the point of coming up with the definitive phrase for characterizing one of the key drawbacks of his approach – 'paralysis by analysis'.

It is all too easy in these more turbulent times to dismiss Ansoff's highly structured methodologies as the product of a rational mind operating in a stable business environment, and therefore of marginal relevance to sophisticated twenty-first century organizations. This would be unfair. Ansoff gave form and structure to organizational thinking

---

Strategy defined by Igor Ansoff

'Strategic management is a comprehensive procedure which starts with a strategic diagnosis and guides a firm through a series of additional steps which culminate in new products, markets and technologies, as well as new capabilities.'

Taken from *Corporate Strategy* (revised edition, 1988)

---

about strategy, and the underlying questions he explored in *Corporate Strategy* – where to grow, how to assess organizational capability, which competencies to leverage, and so on – are crucial issues that need to be faced by any organization seeking to build its future.

The author

Born in Vladivostock in 1918, Igor Ansoff spent his early years in Moscow. After the Ansoff family arrived in New York in 1936, Ansoff trained as an engineer and mathematician. He worked for the Rand Corporation before joining the Lockheed Corporation, where he rose to become Vice President of Planning and Programs.

In 1963, he made the move into academia. He is now Distinguished Professor of Strategic Management at the US International University in San Diego. He is also President of Ansoff Associates, and sits on the board of Gemini Consulting.

Sources and further reading

Igor Ansoff, 1965, *Corporate Strategy*, McGraw Hill, New York.

Igor Ansoff, 'A profile of intellectual growth', in *Management Laureates*, JAI Press, London, 1994.

Igor Ansoff, Roger Declerck and Roger Hayes, 1976, *From Strategic Planning to Strategic Management*, John Wiley, New York.

Igor Ansoff, 1957, 'Strategies for Diversification', *Harvard Business Review*.

ROBERT BALDOCK

The Last Days of the Giants?

2000

'Size matters' proclaimed posters advertising the 1998 movie *Godzilla*. And certainly the latest wave of mergers, acquisitions, and strategic alliances seem to suggest that the future belongs to the corporate giants. On the other hand, the view that big is beautiful has looked less and less convincing in recent times as corporate giants have consistently been upstaged and outthought by smaller, nimbler rivals.

Robert Baldock sees major problems ahead for those organizations that have come to believe that their sheer size will protect them from the unpredictability of the next few years. 'The environment in which the culture of "bigness" blossomed is fast disappearing in many industries', he says.

However, the question mark in the title of Baldock's book is significant – the corporate giants of the late twentieth century may be in serious trouble, but he believes that they can survive in the intensely competitive environment of the twenty-first century if they radically alter the way they do things. He highlights three areas in particular where the giants may need to change their outlook. These are:

1 *The nature of what they offer to their customers.* Most companies have traditionally sold products or services to their customers. Increasingly, companies will need to think in terms of selling solutions and, beyond that, of satisfying customer intentions. An intention, explains Baldock, is 'a desire or goal that may take a person many years to achieve and may involve the integration of products and solutions from multiple firms spanning many industries. For example, "Having an enjoyable retirement" could involve a move to a sunny climate, a new hobby, making financial provisions for your

nearest and dearest, and so on.' The further a company can move away from simply selling products and services towards providing solutions and satisfying intentions, the better it will be able to differentiate its offerings from those of the competition.

2 *The nature of the relationship they have with their customers.* Is the business seller-driven, customer-centred, or buyer driven? Historically, large organizations have presumed to know what the market might want to buy. More recently, the world has become more customer-centred, with sellers trying to tailor their offerings to meet fast-changing consumer needs. Baldock predicts that 'we are entering a buyer-driven era, an era in which the customer will not just be a king, but a dictator'. More than just an extreme form of the customer-centred model, Baldock suggests that in a buyer-driven world, sellers may not have direct contact with consumers but might have to deal with a trusted intermediary selected by the consumer. These intermediaries will in effect invite selected sellers to bid for the business. There is no room in such a market for producers to draw any conclusions in advance about what customers might want.

3 *Their level of virtualization.* At the first level, the company tries to do everything in-house. At the second, the company selectively outsources work to third parties. Beyond the outsourcing model lies the virtual enterprise, carrying very few processes itself and concentrating its efforts of organizing the efforts of others. Baldock defines virtualization as 'the removal of constraints of form, place and time made possible by the convergence of computing, communications and content'.

Combining these three elements, the optimal twenty-first century organization, says Baldock, will be a buyer-driven virtual enterprise that satisfies consumer intentions.

His prescription for big business survival involves three stages:

- firstly, companies should re-assess the economics of sales and delivery channels with a view to dumping excess baggage;
- secondly, they should move to a more customer-centred business model 'where their pared-down products and distribution channels are integrated and closely aligned with the key buyer values of their customer segments'; and
- finally, they must turn their business model through 180 degrees in order to come up with value-creating packages that satisfy consumer intentions.

Whether Baldock truly has come up with a route map for big business survival is open to question, but *The Last Days of the Giants?* is necessary bed-time reading for any large company CEO whose business is in danger of being taken to the cleaners by upstart competitors.

Reality check

Although Baldock believes that large companies can survive over the coming decades, he is realistic enough to acknowledge that there are several forces that are working against industrial gigantism. Among the most significant are:

- New firms that are more agile and innovative than the giants. The internet is helping to put small agile newcomers on a par with large corporations and able to compete head on with them for new business. Just as Microsoft could appear from virtually nowhere to usurp the market of mighty IBM, so a few years later Netscape appeared overnight and threatened to undermine the market (and the size) of Microsoft. In this world, small, agile firms have an advantage over giant organizations, which are unable to take decisions quickly.
- A shift in power from the seller to the buyer. The convergence of computing, communications and content in the shape of personal computers hooked up over a network to the internet has triggered a revolution in the way business is conducted. Users of these technologies have 24-hour access to almost everything, everywhere. Internet-based search agents make it possible for these users to track down the cheapest products in seconds, and new internet-based intermediaries (the so-called 'infomediaries') have created a new form of commerce whereby the buyer sets the price, not the seller.
- Changing government attitudes towards the giants. Governments have become less enchanted with big business. They have stopped mergers from going ahead and have sought to break up some of the larger firms to create more competition. Through a programme of deregulation they have also forced the large players to focus more on the needs of their customers and to drop their prices.
- Industry convergence. Many large companies are moving into new markets (retailers into financial services, for example). They are doing this for one of two reasons: either because their own markets give them little scope for growth; or as part of a drive to hang onto their most profitable customers by offering them a broader range of

products and services. In both cases, these assaults on new markets are being made with new products or services at incredibly low prices.

- A very short-term focus. Institutional investors and brokers' analysts have become very demanding of public companies. In the US in particular, they relentlessly demand an improvement in results every quarter. Fail to deliver against this expectation and top managers are out, regardless of their past track record. Against this backdrop, companies have become reluctant to make large, long-term investments for fear of damaging their short-term results.

These five forces have led to the most competitive environment in the history of commerce, and they spell big trouble for the giants which may have become too big to respond quickly to the threats that they pose.

(Derived from *The Last Days of the Giants*)

Is your company too big for its boots?

Baldock offers readers this simple test: if you can positively identify with any of the following statements:

- 'current mergers and acquisitions activity will continue unabated well into the twenty-first century';
- 'flashy internet start-ups cannot threaten our core activities built up over years of careful planning, research, branding and marketing';
- 'our sheer size will protect us from the unpredictability of the next few years';
- 'we shall manage our customers; they will not manage us';
- 'the government will always have the best interests of big business at heart';
- 'a long-term focus is the key to success';
- 'we do not see the value of outsourcing';
- 'just because we are big, it doesn't mean we cannot move quickly';

then you and your company may be in very serious trouble.

The author

Robert Baldock is Chief Executive of @speed, an organization that aims to help people save time and improve their quality of life. He was previously a global managing partner with Andersen Consulting, which he joined in 1976 at the age of 21, before going on in 1987 to become one of the youngest people ever to become a partner in the firm. In his spare time, he is Chairman of the UK Motorsport Industry Association, the trade body representing British motorsport.

Sources and further reading

Robert Baldock, 2000, *The Last Days of the Giants?* John Wiley, New York.

SHONA BROWN
& KATHLEEN EISENHARDT

Competing on the Edge

1998

C *ompeting on the Edge* was one of the first books that attempted to translate leading-edge complexity concepts from science into management practice. It concludes, perhaps not surprisingly given its background, that organizations need to move from a static strategic proposition (grounded in analytical rigour and standard techniques) to a more dynamic fluid model that draws its energy from the boundaries of chaos. For those readers who are not familiar with complexity theory, the edge of chaos is a key concept which suggests that systems that exist at the boundary zone between chaos and stability are most capable of evolving to meet (continually) emerging new orders.

According to Brown and Eisenhardt, the edge of chaos is characterized by:

- The existence of a few rules (like priorities) that are not arbitrary and are not compromises between extreme values. They are specific rules that can create, for example, the flocking behaviour of birds.
- The need to maintain the balance on the edge of chaos because it is a 'dissipative equilibrium' (i.e. in a constant state of flux and therefore unstable). There is a constant tendency to fall into the attractors of structure and chaos.
- Surprise. Expect the unexpected because control is not tight and because the system is adapting in real time to unpredictable changes.
- Mistakes. These occur because systems at the edge of chaos often slip off the edge. But there is also quick recovery, and, like jazz musicians who play the wrong note, there is a chance to turn mistakes into advantages.

They go on to propose that companies competing successfully 'on the edge' use four main approaches to creating strategy:

1 Management teams build collective intuition through frequent meetings and real-time metrics that enhance their ability to see threats and opportunities early and accurately. Less successful teams rarely meet with their colleagues in a group and make fewer and larger strategic choices, relying on market analyses and future trend projections that are idiosyncratic to the decision.

2 Executives stimulate conflict by assembling diverse teams, challenging them through mindset-breaking tactics, such as scenario planning and role playing, and stressing multiple alternatives to improve the quality of decision making. Less successful performers move quickly to a few alternatives, analyse the best ones, and make a speedy decision.

3 Effective decision-makers focus on maintaining decision pace, not pushing decision speed. They sustain momentum through the methods of time pacing, prototyping, and consensus with qualification. Ineffective decision-makers stress the rarity and significance of strategic choices. Because the decision then looms large, they oscillate between procrastination and 'shotgun' strategic choices against deadlines.

4 Managers on successful teams take a negative view of politicking. Their perspective is collaborative, not competitive. These teams emphasize common goals, clear turf, and having fun. Less effective decision-makers have a competitive orientation and lack a sense of teamwork.

There is much in this book that is fascinating and it makes an excellent read. The authors use a wealth of case studies, interviews, and examples to illustrate the practical implications of this for business today.

However, the book falls short of offering a convincing new view of the strategic process. Instead, it offers many insights into how organizations will need to adapt and change to meet the challenges of an ever more complex environment where the intangible increasingly takes precedence over the tangible.

Perhaps this is because the authors rely on a definition of strategy that is too narrow. They assert that strategy is about two things – deciding where you want your business to go and figuring out how to get there. But, most important of all, strategy is about figuring out *where you are* in the first place, which also implies knowing *who* you are.

Zeitbite: Ten rules for competing on the edge

1. Advantage is temporary: treat any strategy as temporary. Understand that competitive advantage is fleeting, and focus on continuously generating new sources of advantage.
2. Strategy is diverse, emergent and complicated: managers who compete on the edge let strategy emerge and then shape and articulate it.
3. Re-invention is the goal: recognize that profitable fortresses are rare and that re-invention is the smarter path to long-term profitability.
4. Live in the present: use just enough structure to stop things from falling apart. Keep businesses poised for change. Keep aware of new opportunities.
5. Stretch out the past: use experience cannily, whilst being wary of becoming locked into outdated competitive models.
6. Reach into the future: launch more experimental products and services, create more strategic alliances, and employ more futurists than your competitors.
7. Time pace change: pace change in the business with the passage of time – don't be driven solely by the occurrence of events.
8. Grow the strategy: let strategy grow and evolve organically – don't try to assemble it all once.
9. Drive strategy from the business level: too much changes too fast to wait for strategy to trickle down through a rigid hierarchy.
10. Repatch businesses to markets and articulate the whole: continually re-examine the make-up of individual businesses and their matches with markets.

(Derived from *Competing on the Edge*)

In a very real sense, this book is concerned with furthering our understanding of the mechanics of change rather than tackling the more fundamental, and often metaphysical, questions that underlie an understanding of the part that we play in co-creating that change. As a result of this missing dimension, it falls short of being a seminal work, although it remains a valuable contribution to management theory.

The authors

Kathleen M Eisenhardt is professor of strategy and organization at Stanford University. She is widely known for her work on strategy, strategic decision-making, and innovation in rapidly changing and highly competitive markets. Her current research centres on collaboration and competition in the converging computing, telecommunications, and semiconductor industries, from the perspectives of complexity, evolutionary and game theories.

Shona L Brown is a consultant with McKinsey & Co.

Sources and further reading

Shona L Brown and Kathleen M Eisenhardt, 1998, *Competing on the Edge: Strategy as Structured Chaos,* Harvard Business School Press, ⋅ Boston.

Kathleen M Eisenhardt and Donald N Sull, January 2001, 'Strategy as Simple Rules', *Harvard Business Review.*

Eisenhardt and Sull contend that a strategy based on simple well-defined rules is essential given that the new economy's most profound strategic implication is that companies must capture unanticipated, fleeting opportunities in order to succeed. In traditional strategy, advantage comes from exploiting resources or stable market positions. In strategy as simple rules, advantage comes from successfully exploiting these fleeting opportunities. In general terms, managers competing in business can choose from three distinct ways to fight. They can build a fortress and defend it; they can nurture and leverage unique resources; or they can flexibly pursue fleeting opportunities within simple rules.

Shona L Brown and Kathleen M Eisenhardt, 1998, 'Time Pacing: Competing in Markets that Won't Stand Still', *Harvard Business Review.*

Shona L Brown and Kathleen M Eisenhardt, 1997, 'The Art of Continuous Change: Linking Complexity Theory and Time-paced Evolution in Relentlessly Shifting Organizations', *Administrative Science Quarterly.*

Kathleen M Eisenhardt, Jean L Kahwajy, and LJ Bourgeois III, 1997, 'How Teams Have a Good Fight', *Harvard Business Review.*

FRANCES CAIRNCROSS

The Death of Distance

1997

eaders of *The Economist* will be familiar with the work of Frances Cairncross, who has been a senior editor there since 1984. Those who have read her indispensable surveys on the telecommunications industry will know what to expect. Written in the same approachable style that makes a high level of technical knowledge unnecessary, *The Death of Distance* does nothing less than map out how converging communications technology will reshape the economic, commercial and political landscape over the next few years.

This is not another narrowly defined book that simply describes advances in information technology and the communications revolution. Its territory lies in the practical ramifications of these advances for the way in which we work and live. It is a journey into a new world, which tackles the changing nature of organizations, communities, government authority and culture and languages along the way. It is a staggering achievement in synthesis helped, no doubt, by access to the formidable resources of *The Economist*.

Near the start of the book, Cairncross sets outs what she calls 'The Trend-spotter's Guide to New Communications', in which she outlines 30 developments in information and communication technology that will impact on industry and society in the not-so-distant future, before going on to discuss each in depth. Here are some of her developments to watch:

- *The Death of Distance:* distance will no longer determine the cost of communicating electronically. Companies will organize certain types of work in three shifts according to the world's three main time zones.

- *The Fate of Location:* companies will locate any screen-based activity wherever they can find the best bargain of skills and productivity.
- *The Irrelevance of Size:* small companies will offer services that, in the past, only giants could provide. Individuals with valuable ideas will attract global venture capital.
- *More Customized Content:* improved networks will also allow individuals to order 'content for one'.
- *A Deluge of Information:* because people's capacity to absorb new information will not increase, they will need filters to sift, process, and edit it.
- *Increased Value of Brand:* what's hot – whether a product, a personality, a sporting event, or the latest financial data – will attract greater rewards because the potential market will increase greatly. That will create a category of global super-rich, many of them musicians, actors, artists, athletes, and investors.
- *Communities of Practice:* common interests, experiences, and pursuits rather than proximity will bind communities together.
- *The Loose-Knit Corporation:* many companies will become networks of independent specialists; more employees will therefore work in smaller units or alone.
- *More Minnows, More Giants:* on one hand, the cost of starting new businesses will decline, and companies will more easily buy in services so that more small companies will spring up. On the other, communication amplifies the strength of brands and the power of networks.
- *The Proliferation of Ideas:* new ideas and information will travel faster to the remotest corners of the world. Third-world countries will have access to knowledge that the industrial world has long enjoyed.
- *The Shift from Government Policing to Self-Policing:* as content sweeps across national borders, it will be harder to enforce laws banning child pornography, libel and other criminal or subversive material, and those protecting copyright and other intellectual property.
- *The Redistribution of Wages:* low-wage competition will reduce the earning power of many people in rich countries employed in routine screen-based tasks, but the premium for certain skills will grow. People with skills that are in demand will earn broadly similar amounts wherever they live in the world. So income differences within countries will grow; and income differences between countries will narrow.

- *A Market for Citizens:* the greater freedom to locate anywhere and earn a living will hinder taxation. Countries will compete to bid down tax rates and to attract businesses, savers, and wealthy residents.
- *The Rebalance of Political Power:* rulers and representatives will become more sensitive to lobbying and public-opinion polls, especially in established democracies.

In the six years since the book was published, some of the specific, technology-based phenomena that Cairncross predicted have come to pass. Some developing countries, for example, now routinely perform on-line services – monitoring security screens, running help-lines and call centres, writing software, and so forth. Much of the social and political change she anticipated, however, has yet to show through to any meaningful level.

Yet in truth, the value of *The Death of Distance* does not rest in whether Cairncross has a good accuracy rate with her predictions. Like any good history of the future, the value lies more in the extent to which Cairncross manages to challenge assumptions and provoke the reader's thinking. By that measure, most people will find this book well worth reading as a primer for what may lie ahead.

The author

Frances Cairncross is a senior editor at *The Economist*, where she has worked since 1984. She is a governor of the National Institute of Economic and Social Research, and is a presenter on the BBC's *Analysis* programme. Her previous books include *Costing the Earth* and *Green Inc.*

Sources and further reading

Frances Cairncross, 1997, *The Death of Distance,* Orion Publishing, London.

The *Economist* website can be found at http://www.economist.com

MANUEL CASTELLS

The Information Age: Economy, Society and Culture

Volume I: *The Rise of the Network Society,* 1996

Volume II: *The Power of Identity,* 1997

Volume III: *End of Millennium,* 1998

K evin Kelly, writing in *New Rules for the New Economy*, describes Manuel Castells as 'a sociologist with a European's bent for the large-scale sweep of history'. In an age when all too many business texts stretch a meagre handful of barely original insights beyond breaking point, Castell's sprawling, literate, visionary and densely-argued trilogy is like trading up from the bargain red plonk in the local supermarket to a classy Bordeaux direct from the vineyard. It's rich, complex, and improving with age.

In *The Rise of the Network Society,* the first of three linked investigations of contemporary global, economic, political and social change, he offers a catalogue of evidence for the arrival of a new global, networked-based culture. For Castells, the Network Society is characterized by, amongst other things:

- the globalization of strategically decisive economic activities;
- the networking form of organization; and
- the flexibility and instability of work, and the individualization of labour.

The book goes on to examine the processes of globalization that have marginalized whole countries and peoples by leaving them excluded from informational networks.

Some of his specific findings are:

- that there is no systematic structural relationship between the diffusion of information technologies and the evolution of unemployment levels in the economy as a whole;
- that although the communications revolution enables the global distribution of major events, particularly sporting set pieces like the Olympics or the World Cup, in general we do not live in a global village but rather in customized cottages, globally produced and locally distributed;
- that the multimedia world is increasingly populated by two distinct populations – the interacting and the interacted, i.e. those who are able to select their communication options and those who are provided with a restricted number of pre-packaged choices; and
- that the new global economy and the emerging informational society are spawning a new urban form – mega-cities, cities with populations of anything from ten million to twenty million. Size, though, is not their defining quality; rather their significance rests in their capacity to function as nodes of the global economy, concentrating media and political power, acting as magnets for regional resources, and linking up the informational networks.

In Volume II, *The Power of Identity*, Castells gives his account of two conflicting trends shaping the world: globalization and identity. The book describes proactive movements, such as feminism and environmentalism, and reactive movements that build trenches of resistance on behalf of God, nation, ethnicity, family or locality. The final volume of the trilogy, *End of Millennium*, is devoted to processes of global social change induced by interaction between networks and identity.

Having studiously refused for virtually all of the three volumes to engage in futurology, Castells concludes the final volume by setting out 'some trends that may configure society in the early twenty-first century'. His key predictions are that we may well see:

- the information technology revolution accelerating its transformative potential, and as a result technology will achieve its potential to unleash productivity;
- the full flowering of the genetic revolution;
- the continuing and relentless expansion of the global economy;
- the survival of nation states, but not necessarily their sovereignty;

Zeitbite

'The twenty-first century will not be a dark age. Neither will it deliver to most people the bounties promised by the most extraordinary technological revolution in history. Rather, it may well be characterized by informed bewilderment.'

Manuel Castells, *The Information Age*

- the 'exclusion of the excluders by the excluded', i.e. those who do not have the capability to participate in the information economy will become more tribal in outlook.

Although Castells voices a number of concerns throughout the three volumes of *The Information Age*, he concludes his trilogy on a cautiously optimistic note: 'Our economy, society, and culture are built on interests, values, institutions, and systems of representation that, by and large, limit collective creativity, confiscate the harvest of information technology, and deviate our energy into self-destructive confrontation. This state of affairs must not be. There is no eternal evil in human nature. There is nothing that cannot be changed by conscious, purposive social action, provided with information, and supported by legitimacy. If people are informed, active, and communicate throughout the world; if business assumes its social responsibility; if the media become the messengers, rather than the message; if political actors react against cynicism, and restore belief in democracy; if culture is reconstructed from experience; if humankind feels the solidarity of the species throughout the globe; if we assert inter-generational solidarity by living in harmony with nature; if we depart for the exploration of our inner self, having made peace among ourselves. If all this is made possible by our informed, conscious, shared decision, while there is still time, maybe then we may, at last, be able to live and let live, love and be loved'.

How then to sum up this trilogy? First of all, it has to be said that Castells is not an easy or quick read – he is a large-canvas thinker, the three books run to almost 1500 pages, and the text and style often fit what you might expect from a European academic! That said, and even if he goes occasionally into over-exhaustive detail, Castells writes with intelligence and obvious insight. For a systematic interpretation of the global information economy world at the turn of the millennium, Castells has no equal.

The author

Recognized as one of the world's leading social thinkers and researchers, Manuel Castells is professor of sociology and of planning at the University of California, Berkeley, where he was appointed in 1979. Prior to this, he spent twelve years teaching at the University of Paris. He has published over 20 books. Castells was born in Spain in 1942.

Sources and further reading

Manuel Castells, *The Information Age: Economy, Society and Culture*, Blackwell Publishers Ltd, Oxford
Volume I: *The Rise of the Network Society*, 1996
Volume II: *The Power of Identity*, 1997
Volume III: *End of Millennium*, 1998

Castells has contributed a highly readable 22-page essay entitled 'Information Technology and Global Capitalism' to a collection edited by Will Hutton and Anthony Giddens called *On the Edge: Living with global capitalism*, Jonathan Cape, London, 2000.

ALFRED CHANDLER

Strategy and Structure

1962

ulitzer Prize-winning business historian Alfred Chandler was one of the seminal influences on the development of thinking about strategy in the 1950s and 1960s. He was one of the first writers, and certainly the first historian, to argue the importance of strategy in the development, management and success of the corporation.

Drawing on his research into the performance of major US companies between 1850 and 1920, and on intensive studies of four 'modern' companies – du Pont, General Motors, Standard Oil, and Sears Roebuck – Chandler's central thesis in *Strategy and Structure* is that strategy gives companies focus and allows them to determine what should be done and why. Once a company has established what its strategy should be, it then needs to ensure that it has the appropriate structure to enable it to achieve its strategy. Chandler put it succinctly: 'structure follows strategy'.

At the time, Chandler's influence was immense. Senior management teams in most major US corporations came to recognize strategy as a major responsibility. By the early 1970s, the largest corporations in the world had strategy departments. He is also credited with having a significant impact on the number of large organizations that chose to decentralize in the 1960s and 1970s as a result of the praise he heaped in his book on Alfred Sloan's decentralization of General Motors back in the 1920s.

In addition, Chandler's work spawned the first strategy consulting firms. Before the 1960s, McKinsey & Co. concentrated on restructuring organizations, rather than on strategy development. Only when Chandler made the explicit connection between strategy and structure did

Strategy defined by Alfred Chandler

'The determination of the long-term goals and objectives of an enterprise, and the adoption of courses of action and the allocation of resources necessary for carrying out these goals.'

Taken from *Strategy and Structure*

consultancies like McKinsey & Co. and the Boston Consulting Group reflect that connection in nature and focus of their consultancy work.

In more recent times, the Chandler idea – that strategy is set and then structure follows – has been questioned. Tom Peters, writing in his book *Liberation Management*, is characteristically blunt: 'I think he [Chandler] got it exactly wrong for it is the structure of the organization that determines, over time, the choices that it makes about the markets it attacks'.

Richard Pascale, in his book *Managing on the Edge*, also takes Chandler's thinking to task: 'The underlying assumption is that organizations act in a rational, sequential manner. Yet most executives will readily agree that it is often the other way around. The way a company is organized, whether functional focused or driven but independent divisions, often plays a major role in shaping its strategy. Indeed, this accounts for the tendency of organizations to do what they know best how to do – regardless of deteriorating success against the competitive realities.'

Peters and Pascale are by no means lone voices. Increasingly, economists and business management professors around the world are taking the view that an organization's culture, heritage and knowledge, and its financial and competitive circumstances, all have a big influence on the development of strategy.

Chandler's thinking, then, makes absolute sense in clear, static markets. In the ambiguous, dynamic, inter-connected markets of the twenty-first century, the octogenarian historian's book serves to remind us of more sedate times rather than necessarily inform our understanding of current strategic issues.

That said, Chandler's book is a meticulously researched and assembled, rigorously argued theoretical masterpiece. Forty years on from its first publication, it remains the best-written strategy book on the management bookshelves.

The author

Alfred duPont Chandler was born in Delaware in 1918. After graduating from Harvard, he served in the US Navy before joining MIT in 1950, where he spent four years as a research associate and professor in history. He subsequently became professor of history at Johns Hopkins University. He became Straus Professor of Business History at Harvard Business School in 1971 (emeritus from 1989).

Sources and further reading

Alfred Chandler, 1962, *Strategy and Structure: Chapters in the History of the Industrial Enterprise*, Doubleday, New York.

Alfred Chandler, 2000, *A Nation Transformed by Information: How Information has shaped the United States from Colonial Times to the Present*, Oxford University Press, Oxford.

Alfred Chandler, 2001, *Inventing the Electronic Century: The Epic Story of the Consumer Electronics and Computer Industry*, Free Press, New York.

In this book, Chandler adds the influence of prior knowledge and capabilities as factors influencing the role of strategy and management in defining the activities of the firm.

JAMES COLLINS & JERRY PORRAS

Built to Last

1994

When *Built to Last* appeared in 1994, it was the product of a six-year investigation by James Collins and Jerry Porras, both Stanford professors at the time, which set out to uncover the underlying principles that could yield enduring, great companies. For the book, they examined eighteen companies that had significantly outperformed the general stock market over a number of decades. The companies looked at included Disney, General Electric, Hewlett-Packard, IBM, and Wal-Mart.

The key finding to emerge from their research was that, in their words, 'the fundamental distinguishing characteristic of the most enduring and successful corporations is that they preserve a cherished core ideology while simultaneously stimulating progress and change in everything that is not part of their core ideology. Put another way, they distinguish their timeless core values and enduring core purpose (which should never change) from their operating practices and business strategies (which should be changing constantly in response to a changing world). In truly great companies, change is a constant, but not the only constant. They understand the difference between what should never change and what should be open for change, between what is truly sacred and what is not. And by being clear about what should never change, they are better able to stimulate change and progress in everything else.'

For Collins and Porras, the essence of greatness does not lie in cost-cutting, restructuring, or the pure profit motive. It lies in people's dedication to building companies around a sense of purpose and around core values that infuse work with the kind of meaning that goes beyond just making a profit. Truly great companies, they claim, immerse their people in the core ideology. At Disney, for example, where their workers are 'cast members' rather than employees, the language and day-to-day rituals of the organization act as an ongoing reinforcement of the values of the company.

But the clinching argument for them is in the evidence they found that those companies with a strong core ideology and which opted to make a lasting contribution also make more money than their more pragmatic, short-termist rivals in the end.

Implicit on every page of *Built to Last* is a simple question: why would a company settle for creating something mediocre that does little more than make money, when it could create something outstanding that makes a lasting contribution as well?

Even as Collins and Porras were preparing their findings in the early 1990s, in fact since the 1970s entrepreneurs have followed a Silicon Valley paradigm – a set of assumptions about how to handle a start-up. The model is very simple: come up with a good idea, raise venture capital, grow as quickly as you can, and then go public or sell up. Above all, though, do it at speed. Even 20 years ago, a company that hadn't made it big within seven to ten years was deemed a failure. There was also at that time an ethic of impermanence: the Silicon Valley business culture generally had no expectation that a company would be built to last.

By today's standards of short-termism Silicon Valley-style, that time frame seems positively snail-like. Entrepreneurs like Bill Hewlett and Dave Packard, co-founders of Hewlett-Packard, or Sam Walton, founder of Wal-Mart, look like relics of a bygone business era.

In 2000, aware that much of what was going on in the new economy seems to undermine the validity of the findings of *Built to Last*, James Collins faced the criticism head-on in an article he wrote for *Fast Company* magazine provocatively titled 'Built to Flip'. In the article, he tells a story that gives an insight into the twenty-first century entrepreneurial mindset: 'Not long ago, I gave a seminar to a group of 20 entrepreneurial CEOs who had gathered at my Boulder, Colorado, management lab to learn about my most recent research. I tried to begin with a quick review of *Built to Last* findings, but almost immediately a chorus of objections rang out from the group: "What does building-to-last have to do with what we face today?"'

'Built to Flip' is an intriguing idea. As Collins describes it: 'No need to build a company, much less one with enduring value. Today, it's enough to pull together a good story, to implement the rough draft of an idea, and – presto! – instant wealth ... In the built-to-flip world, the notion of investing persistent effort in order to build a great company seems, well, quaint, unnecessary – even stupid.'

He goes on, 'Have we laboured to build something better than what members of previous generations built – only to find their faces staring back at us in the mirror? Is the biggest flip of all the flip that transforms the once-promising spirit of the new economy back into the tired skin of the old economy?'

Encouragingly, he concludes that Built to Flip is itself not built to last. He puts his faith in a combination of the underlying logic of the market-place and the nature of the human spirit: 'Built to Flip can't last. Ultimately, it cannot become the dominant model. Markets are remarkably efficient: in the long run, they reward actual contribution, even though short-run market bubbles can divert excess capital to non-contributors. Over time, the marketplace will crush any model that does not produce real results. Its self-correcting mechanisms will ensure the brutal fairness on which our social stability rests.'

Let's hope that Collins is right. Let's hope that founders of new economy businesses come to realize that it is better to concentrate primarily on building an organization rather than on hitting a market just right with a visionary product idea and riding the growth curve of an attractive product cycle. Let's hope that the primary output of their efforts is the creation of the company itself and what it stands for. And finally, let's hope that twenty-first century entrepreneurs find value in Collins and Porras's analysis of which corporate cultures worked at the end of the twentieth century, and that they recognize *Built to Last* as a book they cannot ignore as they evolve a post-new-economy strategic lens.

The authors

James Collins runs a management learning laboratory in Boulder, Colorado, and is a visiting professor at the University of Virginia. He has also taught at Stanford and worked at McKinsey & Co. and Hewlett-Packard. He can be contacted at JCC512@aol.com

Jerry I Porras is the Fred H Merrill Professor of Organizational Behaviour and Change at Stanford University Graduate School of Business. He has been based at Stanford since 1972. Prior to that he was in the US Army and worked at Lockheed and General Electric. His contact details are Porras_Jerry@GSB.Stanford.edu

Sources and further reading

James C Collins and Jerry I Porras, 1994, *Built to Last*, Harper Business, New York.

James C Collins, March 2000, 'Built to Flip', *Fast Company*, Issue 32.

James C Collins and Jerry I Porras, September/October 1996, 'Building Your Company's Vision', *Harvard Business Review*.

STAN DAVIS
& CHRISTOPHER MEYER

Blur

1998

I n recent years, as the world has grown ever more complicated and confusing, business books have started to lose their sense of certainty. From *The Principles of Scientific Management* by Frederick Taylor, published in 1911, to *Competitive Strategy* by Michael Porter, which first appeared in 1980, business books carried an air of authority. But just as 'Trust me, I'm a doctor' has lost its convincing resonance in the light of numerous medical scandals, so Taylor's idea of 'the one best way' to tackle management and corporate issues no longer convinces. Management thinkers these days offer paradox instead of paracetamol.

So it is with *Blur*, a book in which Davis and Meyer are absolutely up-front about the state of their thinking: 'We are not offering the ultimate word on our topics, but a starting point: provocative ideas, observations, and predictions to get you to think creatively about your business and your future.'

The authors, who are both based at the Ernst & Young Centre for Business Innovation in Boston, maintain that 'connectivity, speed, and the growth of intangible value' have catapulted business into a period of unprecedented transition that demands immediate and creative attention.

These three elements in combination, say Davis and Meyer, 'are blurring the rules and redefining our businesses and our lives. They are destroying solutions, such as mass production, segmented pricing, and standardized jobs, that worked for the relatively slow, unconnected industrial world.'

Ignore these forces at your peril, they warn. Harness and leverage them, 'and you can enter the world of blur, move to its cadence and once again see the world clearly'. To achieve this clarity, it is necessary to see

---

The Blur Equation

Speed × Connectivity × Intangibles = BLUR

Speed every aspect of business and the connected organization operates and changes in real time;

Connectivity everything is becoming electronically connected to everything else: products, people, companies, countries, everything;

Intangibles every offer has both tangible and intangible economic value. The intangible is growing faster;

BLUR The new world in which you will come to live and work.

(Taken from *Blur*)

---

where the forces of blur are having an impact. The authors explore three particular areas: the blur of desires; the blur of fulfilment; and the blur of resources.

- *The blur of desires*: the demand side of an economy, 'where products and services meld into one to become an offer, and where the roles of buyers and sellers merge into an exchange'. Amazon exemplifies both: buy a book and we'll get it delivered to your door, and you tell us what you think about one book and see what others have made of books you have yet to read.

- *The blur of fulfilment*: 'where strategies and organizations dissolve into economic webs and permeable relationships'. This creates a new economic model in which 'returns increase rather than diminish; supermarkets mimic stock markets; and you want the market – not your strategy – to price, market and manage your offer.'

- *The blur of resources*: 'where people are no longer divided into their working and consuming selves, and where capital is more often a liability than an asset. These resources are shaking off their traditional meanings as vigorously as a dog shakes off water after climbing out of a lake.' This is demonstrated in the emergence of the idea of intellectual capital as a resource that can be more crucial to a company's survival than more traditional assets. There is also a sense here of the merging of work-life and life-life.

Davis and Meyer give numerous examples of the way in which traditional boundaries between product and service, capital and people, and buyer and seller are now blurred.

Davis and Meyer contend that blurring offers fresh challenges that should help companies thrive in a changing environment. To help companies and individuals come to terms with operating in a blurred world, they conclude their book by distilling their ideas into '50 ways to BLUR your business'. Some examples are: Make speed your mindset; Connect everything with everything; Grow your intangibles faster than your tangibles; Manage all business in real time; Be able to do anything you do at anytime, anyplace; Put your offer on-line and make it interactive; Customize every offer; Don't grow what you can buy; Assume everything will be deregulated; Be big and small simultaneously; Use it, don't own it. If you do own it, use it up; Prize intellectual assets most, financial assets second, physical assets least; and Pay attention – attention is the next scarce resource

They also have some advice for individuals, recommending that we should consider it carefully. Their ten ways to blur yourself include gie away knowledge to get more back; create something new constantly; sell your value on the web; let the market, not the company, determine your worth; become a free agent while still on a payroll; and brand yourself – there's equity there.

There are, then, very positive steps that we can take, organizationally and individually, in order to negotiate the blurred world successfully. That standing still and doing nothing seems to be the most dangerous response of all is a paradox that Davis and Meyer would probably relish.

The authors

Stan Davis is a Massachusetts-based writer and speaker. He is senior research fellow at the Ernst & Young Centre for Business Innovation in Cambridge, Massachusetts.

Christopher Meyer is the Director of the Centre for Business Innovation, a Partner in Ernst Young, and President of Bios GP, a venture that applies complexity theory to business.

Sources and further reading

Stan Davis and Christopher Meyer, 1998, *Blur: The Speed of Change in the Connected Economy*, Addison-Wesley, New York.

Stan Davis and Christopher Meyer, 2000, *Future Wealth*, Harvard Business School Press, Boston.

Stan Davis, 1996, *Future Perfect (10th anniversary edition)*, Addison Wesley, New York.

LARRY DOWNES & CHUNKA MUI

Unleashing the Killer App

1998

Q: What do longbows, light bulbs, Model Ts and atomic bombs have in common?
A: They are all inventions whose impact has extended far beyond the activities for which their creators made them. They are killer apps.

Downes and Mui define a killer app as 'a new good or service that establishes an entirely new category and, by being first, dominates it, returning several hundred percent on the initial investment ... Killer apps are the Holy Grail of technology investors, the stuff of which their silicon dreams are made.'

For most companies, killer apps are viewed with mixed feelings. Like as not, say the authors, 'killer apps wind up displacing unrelated older offerings, destroying and re-creating industries far from their immediate use, and throwing into disarray the complex relationships between business partners, competitors, customers, and regulators of markets'.

Killer apps have the potential to earn enormous sums of money and to re-energize stale economic sectors. But, warn Downes and Mui, 'like the Hindu god Shiva, they are both regenerative and destructive. It is not for nothing that they are called killer apps.' Companies, they go on, are 'likely to be bumped off'.

Today's killer apps spring mainly from the digital realm, i.e. from the transformation of information into digital form, where it can be manipulated by computers and transmitted by networks. Over the past ten years, the world-wide web, personal computers, e-mail and, most recently, mobile phone technology have reshaped (and will continue to influence profoundly) both our working and the social worlds in ways that we are still grappling to come to terms with.

The driving force behind killer apps is the remarkable science of semiconductors, which has shifted the world's economy from an industrial to an information base in a little over a quarter of a century. Against this backdrop, Downes and Mui claim that a combination of two laws is driving the proliferation of killer apps – Moore's Law and Metcalfe's Law:

'The unrelenting, exponential improvements in semiconductor speed, size, and cost that have operated since the 1960s follow Moore's Law, a prediction by Intel founder Gordon Moore that every 18 months, for the foreseeable future, chip density (and hence computing power) would double while cost remained constant, creating ever more powerful computing devices without raising their price ... Moore's Law may even underpredict the improvement for the next several years. Similar phenomena have been observed by Gordon Bell in data storage and communications bandwidth. The bottom line is simple but potent: faster, cheaper, smaller.

'Less well known than Moore's Law is the observation made by Robert Metcalfe, founder of 3Com Corporation, that networks (whether of telephones, computers, or people) dramatically increase in value with each additional node or user. Metcalfe's Law values the utility of a network as the square of the number of its users, and can be easily appreciated by considering the impact of standard railroad gauges, Morse code, and standardized electrical outlets in the last century, and telephones, fax machines, and internet protocols today. Once a standard has achieved critical mass, its value to everyone multiplies exponentially.'

Moore's Law and Metcalfe's Law both found their apotheosis in the internet. Moore provided the computing power to create new applications, and Metcalfe the growth hormone to extend the level of participation.

These two laws are fundamentally changing the way businesses interact with each other and with their customers. Software companies, for example, habitually make new products and standards available at no cost via the internet in order to reach critical mass more quickly. The business logic is straightforward: achieving critical mass today predisposes future users to adopt products with increased enthusiasm and thereby opens up access to potential marginal revenue. Another example of the two laws in tandem is the growth of computing devices with internet connections – video games, personal digital assistants, mobile phones and the like: users beget users.

Against this backdrop, organizations, from entrepreneurial start-ups to mega-corporations, are coming to realize that the killer-app universe will only accommodate two groups – those that master or nurture killer apps and those that fall victim to them. Not surprisingly, Downes and Mui commend membership of the former group and in the book outline twelve points (see the boxed panel) for designing a digital strategy to help identify and create killer apps in an organization.

Implicit in their concept of digital strategy is a view that the classical approach to strategy – top-down, analytical, based on a thorough understanding of the marketplace, executing carefully developed plans over a period of time – has little place in a killer-app universe. Digital strategy has two guiding principles: the first is that the best way to predict the future is to invent it, and the second suggests that the future is unknowable beyond – at most – a 12–18-month time frame, that strategy therefore needs to become a real-time, dynamic, intuitive process.

Downes and Mui have some convincing advice about how to prosper in the digital world. But below the surface there is a more disquieting message: that no matter what your company does, or its size, or its market position, there's probably a killer app lurking out there somewhere that will redefine your business world.

The 12 principles of killer app design

Reshaping the landscape

1 *Outsource to the customer:* e.g. build an interface into your information sources and give customers the tools to navigate and customize them. Customers provide you with their data – it's more accurate and cheaply gathered.

2 *Cannibalize your markets*: on-line newspapers for example may reduce sales of print editions, but this loss is balanced against the unrealized power of other information assets that can be exploited in cyberspace.

3 *Treat each customer as a market segment of one*: cyberspace lends itself to mass customization.

4 *Create communities of value*: nurture relationships both with and between customers.

Building new connections

5   *Replace rude interfaces with learning interfaces*: e.g. by giving the customers what they want rather than what they would accept.

6   *Ensure continuity for the customer, not yourself:* customers don't know or don't care when technology replaces familiar ways of doing things as the interface looks the same, e.g. digital gauges on car dashboards.

7   *Give away as much information as you can*: the age of closed information systems is over.

8   *Structure every transaction as a joint venture*: e.g. larger organizations need to learn how to buy, sell, partner and compete with a new breed of virtual firms.

Redefining the interior

9   *Treat your assets as liabilities*: reduce physical assets, build up intangible assets.

10   *Destroy your value chain*: ... before your competitors do. Pay particular attention to the declining need for intermediaries.

11   *Manage innovation as a portfolio of options:* retain flexibility about the best ideas and the best way to implement them.

12   *Hire the children*: they are the natives of cyberspace – incorporate their values, energy and mindset into your thinking.

(Derived from *Unleashing the Killer App*)

The authors

Born in 1959, Larry Downes is a consultant with 20 years' experience of working with global businesses. He also teaches law and technology at Northwestern University.

Chunka Mui is Executive Editor of the business magazine *Context* and a partner with Diamond Technology Partners. He is also Director of the Diamond Exchange, a forum for exploring issues in digital strategy.

Sources and further reading

Larry Downes and Chunka Mui, 1998, *Unleashing the Killer App: Digital strategies for market dominance,* Harvard Business School Press, Boston.

Downes and Mui have developed a companion website, which allows budding digital strategists to communicate and share thinking around the globe. Bearing in mind Metcalfe's Law, www.killer-apps.com may well grow to be a more vital resource than the book.

PETER DRUCKER
The Age of Discontinuity
1969

*T*he Age of Discontinuity* begins with an attention-grabbing act of historical imagination: 'No one knowing only the economic facts and figures of 1968 and of 1913 – and ignorant both of the years in between and of anything but economic figures – would even suspect the cataclysmic events of this century, such as two world wars, the Russian and Chinese Revolutions, or the Hitler regime. They seem to have left no traces in the statistics.'

It's typically Drucker – provocative, literate and intelligent. His central thesis was that – despite a number of momentous world events – society, the economy and business had been reasonably stable throughout much of the twentieth century. This he attributed to the 'fulfilment of the economic and technological promises of the Victorian and Edwardian eras'.

But *The Age of Discontinuity*, first published in 1969, was not about the past, it was about the future, a future that Drucker predicted would be characterized by discontinuity rather than continuity. Anybody reading the book today will be struck by how accurately Drucker portrayed the future. It is a remarkable act of economic, technological, political and cultural prediction.

We shouldn't be surprised. After all, Drucker has spent 50 years proving himself to be most prescient business-trend spotter of our time. Back in the 1950s, he was describing how computer technology would transform business. In 1961, he predicted the impending rise of Japan as an economic power. He was the first to coin concepts of 'management by objectives', 'privatization' and 'knowledge workers', and many others besides.

The Age of Discontinuity was originally published in 1969 (an updated preface was added in the 1983 edition, noting that the earlier

Zeitbites

Peter Drucker chronicles the rise of the knowledge worker, 1954–1969

'In the United States ... the class of employees that has been growing most rapidly in numbers and proportion is that of skilled and trained people.'

The Practice of Management, 1954
'Productive work in today's society and economy is work that applies vision, knowledge and concepts – work that is based on the mind rather than the hand.'

Landmarks of Tomorrow, 1959
'Even the small business today consists increasingly of people who apply knowledge rather than manual skill and muscle to work.'

Managing for Results, 1964
'Every knowledge worker in a modern organization is an "executive" if, by virtue of his position or knowledge, he is responsible for a contribution that materially affects the capacity of the organization to perform and to obtain results.'

The Effective Executive, 1966
'Finally, these new industries differ from the traditional "modern" industry in that they will employ predominantly knowledge workers rather than manual workers.'

comments were basically still relevant). The book did not forecast as such, but rather focused with great clarity and perception on the forces of change that were beginning in the late 1960s to transform the economic landscape and creating tomorrow's society.

Drucker discerned four major areas of discontinuity underlying the then social and cultural reality:

- the rapid emergence of new technologies resulting in major new industries;
- the emergence of the global economy;

- a new socio-political reality of pluralistic institutions that would pose drastic political, philosophical and spiritual challenges to government and society; and
- the emergence of knowledge as the new capital and the central resource of the economy, with significant implications for mass education, work, leisure and leadership.

It is in this last area that Drucker has been a commanding presence for half a century. Although he had been writing about the rise of knowledge work and the knowledge worker since 1954, it was in *The Age of Discontinuity* that he first set out a detailed account of the issue.

He foresaw that the rise of knowledge work would inevitably cause significant change in the workplace. He wrote that 'knowledge work itself knows no hierarchy, for there are no "higher" and 'lower' knowledges. Knowledge is either relevant to a given task or irrelevant to it. The task decides, not the name, the age, or the budget of the discipline, or the rank of the individual plying it… Knowledge, therefore, has to be organized as a team in which the task decides who is in charge, when, for what, and for how long.'

Drucker also recognized that the 'knowledge worker' would be a new breed of employee, and would therefore need a more subtle form of management. 'Though the knowledge worker is not a labourer', he wrote, 'and certainly not proletarian, he is not a subordinate in the sense that he can be told what to do; he is paid, on the contrary, for applying his knowledge, exercising his judgement, and taking responsible leadership.'

The knowledge worker, Drucker predicted, would be a very different creature from the loyal, subservient 'organization man'. He wrote that 'the knowledge worker sees himself just as another professional, no different from the lawyer, the teacher, the preacher, the doctor or the government servant of yesterday. He has the same education. He has more income, he has probably greater opportunities as well. He may well realize that he depends on the organization for access to income and opportunity, and that without the investment the organization has made … there would be no job for him, but he also realizes, and rightly so, that the organization equally depends on him.'

Drucker's foresight extended well beyond the workplace. He recognized that the transition from the industrial age to the information age would profoundly change society, business and government. Knowledge would confer tremendous power on those who possessed it.

The Age of Discontinuity stands up as possibly the most prescient management text of all time. Anyone re-reading this book more than

Beatty on Drucker

'Drucker discusses economic life in terms of values, integrity, character, knowledge, vision, responsibility, self-control, social integration, teamwork, community, competence, social responsibility, the quality of life, self-fulfilment, leadership, duty, purpose, dignity, meaning – but rarely money. He defends profit, but as if it were broccoli: a distasteful obligation of managers who would rather be reading Kierkegaard.'

Jack Beatty, in his book
The World According to Peter Drucker, Free Press, 1998

30 years after its first publication will find it remarkable that Drucker uncovered a future world of work that nobody else detected. The book is a most astonishing achievement, all the more so for the fact that most of his analysis could have been written today.

The author

Born in 1909 in Vienna, Peter Ferdinand Drucker was educated first in Austria and then in England, where he took his doctorate in public and international law. He began his career as a newspaper reporter in Frankfurt. He subsequently worked for various banks and companies in London before moving to America in 1937. He took a succession of academic appointments before moving to California in 1971 to become Clark Professor of Social Science at Claremont Graduate School. He has received honorary degrees from universities in the US, Belgium, Great Britain, Japan, Spain and Switzerland. Now in his nineties, he still writes occasionally for the *Wall Street Journal* and the *Harvard Business Review*.

Sources and further reading

Peter Drucker, 1969, *The Age of Discontinuity*, Heinemann, London.
Peter Drucker, 1999, *Management Challenges for the 21st Century*, HarperCollins, New York.
Peter Drucker, 1993, *Post-Capitalistic Society*, HarperCollins, New York.

An early picture of new economy, which has held up extremely well over the intervening years.

Peter Drucker, 1954, *The Practice of Management*, Harper & Row, New York.

A book of huge range and continuing relevance – the first to explore the concept of Management by Objectives.

PHILIP EVANS & THOMAS S WURSTER

Blown to Bits

2000

T hose in the business of communicating information to others have until now faced a strategic choice, which can be characterized as richness or reach. Providing rich, customized information about a product or service necessarily limited the number of potential customers that could be reached with that information. On the other hand, going for reach necessarily meant that the degree of customization of the information reduced in direct correlation with the widening universe of customers. So, which to go for? This simple yet absolute trade-off has long stood at the centre of the information business.

Indeed, the organization providing the information itself reflects a trade-off between richness and reach – essentially providing a physical infrastructure and established behavioural patterns that enable and govern the sharing of information vital to the work of business.

According to Philip Evans and Thomas S Wurster, two consultants from the Boston Consulting Group, this dilemma is fast disappearing as advanced digital technologies are allowing information to separate from its physical carrier. This, in effect, kills off the richness/reach trade-off and renders many traditional business structures and the strategies that drive them obsolete.

They begin *Blown to Bits* with a case study showing how Microsoft's *Encarta* blew *Encyclopaedia Britannica* out of the water. The multivolume version of the prestigious *Britannica* dominated the encyclopaedia market for most of the twentieth century, with sales reaching a peak of $650 million in 1990. The marketing proposition – educational advantage for your kids at a price – was compelling and successful. Since 1990, sales of printed encyclopaedias have plummeted by 80%, 'blown away by a product of the late-twentieth century information revolution: the CD-ROM'.

Zeitbite

No, we're not in denial

In an interview with Amazon.co.uk, Philip Evans explains how business people get, but don't get, the new economics of information.

Amazon.co.uk: How do most businesspeople respond when you tell them their businesses are about to come unglued?

Evans: I do a lot of speaking, and about a year ago, I gave two speeches in the same week. One was to a group of newspaper executives and the other was to a group of bankers. And I made the Blown to Bits argument for the newspaper audience by talking about banking, and they all agreed. And then, when I said, 'Well, of course, you do realize the same logic applies to you,' they all vigorously disagreed – said that was absolute nonsense. And then, a few days later, talking to the banking audience, I made the argument by using the newspaper industry, and they all agreed: 'Yes, it's obviously true.' And yet, when I said, 'Well, it applies to you, too,' they all similarly said, 'No, that's absolute nonsense.' So while everybody can see the logic in other businesses, it's much harder for them to see it in their own. But I can't help noticing that more recently people have begun to accept that this change is cutting much closer to the core of their business identities than they ever thought.

There are other examples of what the authors call 'the new economics of information'. In the music industry right now, we can witness a lively ongoing struggle around MP3 and related technologies.

This is not just a matter of concern for those working in explicit 'information' businesses. The authors argue that in every industry information is the 'glue' that holds value chains, supply chains, consumer franchises, and organizations together across the entire economy, and go on to illustrate how the melting of this glue has major implications. They describe how the explosion in connectivity and the adoption of common information standards are causing the blow-up of the richness/reach trade-off and radically transforming economic relationships in all their manifestations. A sales force, a system of branches, a printing press, a chain of stores, or a delivery fleet – which once served as formidable barriers to entry because they took years and heavy investment to build – suddenly become expensive liabilities.

As the informational glue that holds these structures together begins to melt, pieces of the business will break apart and recombine in entirely new ways. Insurgent players, newly armed with the ability to provide both richness and reach to customers – and unburdened by cumbersome physical assets – will emerge from nowhere to pick off the most profitable slivers within scores of industries.

This will engender the breaking apart and recombining of traditional business structures. The bad news, say the authors, is that deconstruction is most likely to strike in exactly the area of the business an incumbent can least afford to lose. They go on to explain how leaders can assess the vulnerability of their own businesses and respond. They also describe how a new form of disintermediation, driven by the new economics of information, threatens not just to re-segment markets, but to destroy the intermediary business model entirely.

Blown to Bits is a compelling mix of strategic analysis and practical guidance.

The authors' analysis is convincing, and it really does appear as though the only options available in the new economics of information are to use the 'un-gluing' of industries to establish a competitive advantage or, alternatively, simply to fall apart at the seams.

The authors

Philip Evans is a senior vice president of The Boston Consulting Group in Boston. He can be reached at evans.philip@bcg.com

Thomas S Wurster is a senior vice president of The Boston Consulting Group in Los Angeles. He can be reached at wurster.tom@bcg.com. Evans and Wurster are co-leaders of The Boston Consulting Group's Media and Convergence Practice.

Sources and further reading

Philip Evans and Thomas S Wurster, 2000, *Blown to Bits: How the New Economics of Information Transforms Strategy*, Harvard Business School Press, Boston.

Philip Evans and Thomas S Wurster, November/December 1999, 'Getting real about virtual commerce', *Harvard Business Review.*

Philip Evans and Thomas S Wurster, September/October 1997, 'Strategy and the new economics of information', *Harvard Business Review.*

CHARLES FERGUSON

High Stakes, No Prisoners

1999

W e tend to think of strategy as a predominantly cerebral exercise. This book is about strategy as visceral roller-coaster.

In 1994, consultant and writer Charles Ferguson set up a company called Vermeer Technologies, named after his favourite painter. It was not the easiest of times to launch a start-up in Silicon Valley, with the US emerging gingerly from a recession, a flat stock market, and the internet yet to be taken seriously by those with money to invest. Yet within two years he sold the company to Microsoft for $133 million, in the process making a fortune for himself and his associates.

Vermeer's 'very cool, very big idea' was FrontPage, the first software product for creating and managing a website, which is now bundled with Microsoft Office and boasts several million users worldwide.

Cue another self-congratulatory business book about how somebody made their millions on the market? Actually no. *High Stakes, No Prisoners* gives a 'warts and all' view into the inner workings of Silicon Valley. In one of his most memorable lines, he describes it as a place where 'one finds little evidence that the meek shall inherit the earth'.

Ferguson is unerringly candid throughout the book, naming names of the people he came across – many of them the big movers and shakers in the industry – and saying what he really thinks of them. For example, he describes Netscape CEO Jim Barksdale as having a poor technical grasp, being 'in over his head from day one' at Netscape, yet at the same time displaying 'extraordinary arrogance'. Oracle founder Larry Ellison is 'a notorious womaniser – and a seriously random number'.

Ferguson is very tough on himself, too, owning up to the mistakes his start-up made, and detailing his own shortcomings as a person and a businessman. There can't be many business books around where

---

Zeitbite

Taking Vermeer from zero to hero

'One year earlier, we'd had to fight for months to raise $4 million ... But by the end of September, we had the opposite problem, and it was a very serious problem indeed. Everyone either wanted a piece of our hide or they wanted us dead because we threatened them. And my problems were by no means confined to the outside world. To the contrary, I needed to defend both Vermeer and myself against our investors and our newly hired CEO just as much as against external threats. Events were moving at the speed of light, everything was connected to everything else, and there was essentially nobody I could talk to about it. So these developments brought astonishing highs and great personal fulfilment, but also brutal fights, extreme stress, and painful lessons.

'Even through August, we had been quite secretive. While we had been speaking to potential partners, large customers, and analysts, we did so very selectively, under nondisclosure, and usually without revealing sensitive technology or strategic plans. But by September our product was nearly done, and it was time to announce ourselves to the world. Our timing was perfect; as we had planned, we could launch in the peak of the fall season. We wanted business, and there was no further point in concealing what either we or our product did. Furthermore, it was also time to raise more money. So it was time to show our stuff. When we did the response was, as they say, overwhelming.'

Taken from *High Stakes, No Prisoners*

---

the index lists, under the heading of the author's name, 'mistakes of', 'naïveté of', and 'paranoia of'.

Best of all, *High Stakes, No Prisoners* is an honest, acerbic and extremely funny account of how business really gets done in high technology. For instance, here's Ferguson on doing a start-up: 'Start-ups are the intellectual equivalent of driving a small, fast convertible with the top down, the stereo playing Keith Jarrett, Bach, or J.J. Cale very loud, doing a hundred miles an hour on an empty road at sunset. You might crash, but the experience is visceral, immediate, and intense.' And on venture capitalists: 'Andy Marcuvitz is a heavyset guy who wears badly fitting suits. He has no discernible personality, sense of humour, or compassion – ideal traits for a venture capitalist.'

Taking Vermeer from inception to its sale to Microsoft was, he writes, 'an amazing experience', but he concludes his book by admitting that he thinks 'it will be a while before I run another company again'. Let's hope that it won't be too long before he turns his caustic pen to a subject that is equally fascinating, and to which he can bring just as much insight and humour.

The author

Charles Ferguson has been a consultant to the White House, many agencies of the US government, and some of the world's leading high-tech companies, before founding Vermeer Technologies with Randy Forward in 1993. He has contributed to the *Harvard Business Review*, *The New York Times*, and *Foreign Policy*. He holds a doctorate in political science from Massachusetts Institute of Technology. He can be reached by e-mail at charles@highstakesnoprisoners.com

Sources and further reading

Charles H Ferguson, 1999, *High Stakes, No Prisoners: A winner's tale of greed and glory in the internet wars*, Times Business, New York.
Charles H Ferguson and Charles Morris, 1993, *Computer Wars*, Times Business, New York.
The authors suggest that the power shift from IBM to Microsoft – the consequences of IBM failing to exploit its own inventions and the importance of becoming the industry standard setter – had more to do with IBM committing a series of blunders than with Microsoft doing anything exceptional.

SUMANTRA GHOSHAL & CHRISTOPHER BARTLETT

The Individualized Corporation

1998

I n a series of landmark articles published between November 1994 and May 1995 in the *Harvard Business Review,* Sumantra Ghoshal and Christopher Bartlett set out a new framework for the strategic process – one based on purpose, processes and people rather than the more familiar model of strategy, structure and systems.

The Individualized Corporation takes their thinking further, revealing the emergence of a fundamentally different management philosophy that focuses on the power of the individual as the driver of value creation. The book was the culmination of six years of research and hundreds of interviews with managers in companies such as Intel, ABB, Canon and 3M.

This is not a book that clings to some faddish management theme, but the work of two serious and respected scholars. Ghoshal is based at the London Business School, while Bartlett is a chaired professor at Harvard Business School.

The authors argue that the traditional strategic paradigm, in which organizational structures and systems support strategy, has been replaced by a more humanistic paradigm which relies more heavily on defining the purpose/vision of the organization and developing the skills to meet this vision. The image of the 'organization man' as a cog in the corporate machine, they say, has become not only dated but dangerous. Rather than try to shoehorn their employees into a homogenous corporate mould based on the company's strategy, structure and systems, Ghoshal and Bartlett maintain that managers must focus on developing the unique talents and skills of individuals.

Since their book was published five years ago, their view has gained in ascendancy.

Zeitbite

'If a company is to become an Individualized Corporation, its operating-level managers must evolve from their traditional role as frontline implementers to become innovative entrepreneurs; senior-level managers must convert themselves from administrative controllers to developmental coaches; and top-level executives are forced to see themselves less as their companies' strategic architects and more as their institution builders.'

Taken from *The Individualized Corporation*

For example, the competitiveness of most businesses in retailing and finance, manufacturing and tourism, depends increasingly on the knowledge, ideas and creativity of the people they employ. These are their most valuable assets. Our economies are shifting away from land, machinery and raw materials as the asset base of business to knowledge, ideas and creativity. That shift will require all businesses to ask fundamental questions about how they are owned and managed, how they pay and involve their employees. Andy Law, managing director and guiding spirit of innovative advertising agency St Luke's, likes to remind his colleagues that business must innovate or die, not just the products they make but their organization, ownership and culture.

The Individualized Corporation has something to say and one of its main achievements is that it does so without resorting to the kind of simplified clichés that fill most management books today. It is an intensely practical book that describes not only the 'what' but also the 'how' of building and managing an organization driven by the creativity and talent of the individuals within it. As Ghoshal explained in an interview with *Management Today* in December 1996, 'A lot of managers work long and hard simply to make the inevitable happen ... They just preside over the inevitable. Yet management is all about making things happen that otherwise wouldn't, about making ordinary people produce extraordinary results.'

If you are in need of a breath of fresh air in the cluttered world of management books, this work is highly recommended. You won't find answers to all the human issues that confront the modern organization but you should find plenty to reinforce the cliché from many an annual report that a company's most precious asset really is its people.

The authors

Sumantra Ghoshal holds the chair of strategic leadership at the London Business School and is one of the leading management thinkers in Europe today.

Christopher Bartlett is a chaired professor at Harvard Business School.

Sources and further reading

Sumantra Ghoshal and Christopher Bartlett, 1998, *The Individualized Corporation*, Heinemann, London.

Sumantra Ghoshal and Christopher Bartlett, May/June 1995, 'Changing the Role of Top Management: Beyond Systems to People', *Harvard Business Review*.

Sumantra Ghoshal and Christopher Bartlett, January/February 1995, 'Changing the Role of Top Management: Beyond Structure to Processes', *Harvard Business Review*.

Sumantra Ghoshal and Christopher Bartlett, November/December 1994, 'Changing the Role of Top Management: Beyond Strategy to Purpose', *Harvard Business Review*.

ARIE DE GEUS

The Living Company

1997

hy do so many organizations die young – most before their 50th birthday?

In the early 1980s, Arie de Geus was part of a group at Shell that undertook a study into corporate longevity, looking as their research base specifically at companies that had passed the century mark. The study concluded that these companies bore striking resemblances to one another, having four essential traits in common:

- sensitivity to the environment – a company's ability to learn and adapt;
- cohesion and identity – a company's innate ability to build a community and a *persona* for itself;
- tolerance and decentralization – a company's ability to build constructive relationships with other entities, within and outside itself, and a willingness to experiment; and
- conservative financing – a company's ability to finance its own growth and evolution effectively by retaining resources that enable flexibility.

De Geus calls these companies 'living companies', whose purpose is to fulfil their potential and perpetuate themselves as ongoing communities. This clearly distinguishes them from what he calls 'economic companies', which are in business to produce wealth for a small inner group. He likens managers in living companies to *stewards* who understand that keeping the company alive means handing it over to a successor in at least the same health that it was in when he or she took charge.

He writes, 'A manager of a living company ... must let people grow within a community that is held together by clearly stated values. The manager, therefore, must place commitment to people before assets, respect for innovation before devotion to policy, the messiness of learning before orderly procedures, and the perpetuation of community before all other concerns ... The feeling of belonging to an organization and identifying with its achievements is often dismissed as soft. But case histories repeatedly show that a sense of community is essential for long-term survival.'

De Geus believes that most companies fail because they focus too narrowly on financial performance and pay insufficient attention to themselves as communities of human beings with the potential to learn, adapt and grow. The living company, he says, emphasizes knowledge rather than capital, and adaptability rather than core competencies.

Living companies excel in surviving and adapting in a world that they recognize they cannot control. A policy of tolerance enables a company to diversify without courting disaster; by allowing it to engage continually with its environment without damaging its capacity for growth.

In a powerful analogy, de Geus compares a company whose purpose is to produce wealth for a few people with a static puddle of rainwater, collecting any new drops into its stagnant basin. In contrast, a living company is like a river – turbulent and changing but permanent and always moving forward in continuity.

For de Geus, the ability of organizations and individuals to learn and adapt is *the* crucial skill. He quotes the work of Allan Wilson of the University of California at Berkeley on how species and (by implication) organizations learn. According to Wilson, there are three conditions necessary to aid a species' learning:

- members of the species must have and use the ability to move around and they must flock or move in herds rather than sit individually in isolated territories;
- some members of the species must have the ability to invent new behaviours and skills; and
- the species must have a communication process for transmitting a skill from the individual to the entire community.

The presence of these three conditions serves to accelerate learning in the species as a whole, increasing its ability to adapt quickly to fundamental changes in the environment. Wilson uses the example of robins and blue tits in Great Britain; the entire species of blue tits – which have

Zeitbite

'Every moment of our lives, we instinctively create action plans and programmes for the future anticipating the moment at hand, the next minutes, the emerging hours, the following days, the ongoing weeks and the anticipated years to come – in one part of our mind. This brain activity takes place throughout the daytime, independent of whatever else we are doing. These plans are sequentially organized, as a series of potential actions: "if this happens, I will do that". These are not predictions. They do not pretend to tell what will happen. They are time paths into an anticipated future. Each combines a future hypothetical condition of the environment ("If the train arrives late") with an option for action ("I will take a cab").

'Not only does the brain make those time paths in the prefrontal lobes, it stores them. We visit these futures and remember our visits. We have, in other words, a "memory of the future", continually being formed and optimized in our imagination and revisited time and time again. The memory of the future is an internal process within the brain, related to humans' language ability and perception. It apparently helps us sort through the plethora of images and sensations coming into the brain, by assigning relevance to them. We perceive something as meaningful if it fits meaningfully with a memory that we have made of an anticipated future.'

Taken from *The Living Company*

social systems – learned to break the seals on milk bottles whereas robins – essentially lone territorial birds – did not. Birds that flock learn faster. In a management context, skunk works and management development programmes are excellent opportunities for flocking.

The book is full of thought-provoking examples like these drawn from the worlds of biology, anthropology and psychology, and de Geus deservedly won the Edwin G Booz prize for Most Insightful Management Book back in 1997. It is a little disappointing that his ideas have not yet broken through into the mainstream. Nonetheless, anybody with an interest in organizational learning will find something of value here.

The author

Arie de Geus worked for 38 years at Royal Dutch Shell, where he was heavily involved in developing Shell's scenario planning capability. Now retired, he spends much of his time lecturing throughout the world and advising governments and private institutions.

Sources and further reading

Arie de Geus, 1997, *The Living Company*, Nicholas Brealey, London.
Arie de Geus, March/April 1997, 'The Living Company', *Harvard Business Review.*

MICHAEL GOOLD, ANDREW CAMPBELL & MARCUS ALEXANDER

Corporate-Level Strategy

1994

C *orporate-Level Strategy* was the product of ten years of research by Goold, Alexander and Campbell into corporations in North America, Europe and Japan. The authors, who are all directors at the Ashridge Strategic Management Centre based in London, were particularly interested in large, multi-business organizations and how the parent companies created – or destroyed – value in the businesses making up their organizations.

As part of their research, they calculated the value of a number of multi-business companies and found that in over half the cases they investigated, the value of the component business units exceeded that of the whole corporation. In trying to establish the cause of this phenomenon, they found that size and diversity were not necessarily problems. Most often, the problem was not the range of businesses in the portfolio, but rather the lack of a coherent corporate strategy that would add any value to them.

Goold, Alexander and Campbell proposed a new approach to the management of multi-business companies, based on the goal of what they term the 'parenting advantage', in other words, the 'mother business' should aim to be the best parent for each of the businesses in the corporate portfolio.

From this research, they derived three essential elements to effective corporate parenting:

1   there needs to be clarity about the parent's role;
2   the parent needs to have distinctive characteristics that match the opportunities presented; and
3   there needs to be recognition that each parent will only work well with certain sorts of business. The parent has to possess relevant

---

Zeitbites

Goold, Alexander and Campbell on parents

- 'The quest for parenting advantage underlies the decision of successful multi-business companies and distinguishes them from their less successful rivals.'
- 'A parent that is well suited to address certain opportunities may be ill suited to address others.'
- 'A parent that lacks a clear focus on value creation opportunities in its businesses is more likely to destroy value than to create it.'
- 'The possession of unusually clear and powerful value creation insights is a vital difference between companies that achieve parenting advantage and those that do not.'
- 'The review of corporate strategy may lead to changes either in the parent or in the portfolio of businesses.'
- 'All new corporate strategies involve learning new parenting skills.'
- 'The top managers in the parent are normally the dominant source of value creation or destruction.'

---

skills, resources and other characteristics that allow it to realize value from the opportunity presented.

If these criteria are met, then there is likely to be a positive chemistry between parent and 'child' that results in the 'child' becoming what the authors term a 'heartland business'. This is how they define the term: 'Heartland businesses are ... well understood by the parent; they do not suffer from the inappropriate influence and meddling that can damage less familiar businesses. The parent has an innate feel for its heartland that enables it to make difficult judgements and decisions with a high degree of success.'

Goold, Alexander and Campbell say that a heartland business is not the same as a core business: 'a core business is often merely a business that the company has decided to commit itself to. In contrast, the heartland definition focuses on the fit between a parent and a business: do the parent's insights and behaviour fit the opportunities and nature of this business? Does the parent have specialist skills in assisting this type of business to perform better?'

Goold, Alexander and Campbell are convincing advocates for their concept of parenting advantage and how it can enable corporate parent businesses to create more value in the portfolio of business than would be achieved by any rival. Given the potential prizes to be gained, reading *Corporate-Level Strategy* should be a high priority for any senior executive working in a multi-business organization that is desperately seeking synergy.

The authors

Michael Goold, Andrew Campbell and Marcus Alexander are directors of the Ashridge Strategic Management Centre, London, England. Previously, they were strategy consultants with either the Boston Consulting Group or McKinsey & Co.

Sources and further reading

Michael Goold, Andrew Campbell and Marcus Alexander, 1994, *Corporate-Level Strategy: Creating value in the multi-business company*, John Wiley, New York.

Michael Goold and Andrew Campbell, 2002, *Designing Effective Organizations: How to Create Structured Networks*, John Wiley, New York.

Andrew Campbell and Michael Goold, 1998, *Synergy*, Capstone, Oxford.

Subtitled *Why links between business units often fail and how to make them work*, this is an insightful and penetrating guide to how and under what circumstances a business portfolio can be worth more than the sum of its parts.

ANDREW GROVE

Only the Paranoid Survive

1996

O nce dubbed 'the best manager in the world' by *Fortune* magazine, Andy Grove is also one of the world's best-known business figures. A co-founder of Intel in 1979, he helped the company grow into what it is today – the world's largest computer chipmaker, not to mention the fifth most admired company in America and the seventh most profitable company among the Fortune 500.

Given his substantial managerial achievements at Intel, it would not have been all that surprising if he had produced a book to add to that already over-crowded genre, the self-aggrandising CEO autobiography. In fact, he is relatively restrained in his use of Intel to illustrate his themes, and when he does, it is more often than not to admit to tactical and strategic mistakes made by the company.

Grove has bigger fish to fry. *Only the Paranoid Survive* is a lesson in leadership and strategy that could benefit any manager in any industry. Grove provides a lens through which to view the challenges posed by an ever-changing business environment, and offers a set of strategic tools to help managers recognize and successfully address those changes.

His start-point is the best known and most influential classical strategy analysis model of all – Michael Porter's Five Competitive Forces – which he paraphrases and augments to produce his own version. Grove's six forces affecting a business are:

1   power, vigour and competence of existing competitors;
2   power, vigour and competence of complementors;
3   power, vigour and competence of customers;
4   power, vigour and competence of suppliers;
5   power, vigour and competence of potential competitors; and

6   possibility that what your business is doing can be done in a different way.

'Complementors' are Grove's addition to Porter's original model. These are businesses from which customers buy complementary products e.g. computers need software, software needs computers. He calls complementors 'fellow travellers'. In Intel's case, the company's most significant complementor is Microsoft, which helps explain Grove's vocal support for Bill Gates during the Antitrust hearings.

Groves cites the sixth force, termed 'substitution' by Porter, as 'the most deadly of all' because 'new techniques, new approaches, new technologies can upset the old order, mandate a new set of rules and create an entirely new climate in which to do business'.

A linked concept is what he calls a 10X factor. 'When a Wal-mart moves into a small town', he writes, 'the environment changes for every retailer in that town. A "10X" factor has arrived. When the technology for sound in movies became popular, every silent actor and actress personally experienced the "10X" factor of technological change.'

A '10X factor' brings massive change into the dynamics of an industry. Examples include the first on-line bank, Amazon's entry into the book market, and the mobile phone.

If '10X' factors are the drivers of massive change, strategic inflection points (SIPs) are those moments in the life history of a business when such change occurs. During an SIP, Grove writes, 'the way a business operates, the very structure and concept of the business, undergoes a change. But the irony is that at that point itself nothing much happens. That subtle point is like the eye of the hurricane ... when it moves the wind hits you again. That is what happens in the middle of the transformation from one business model to another.'

SIPs are his 'big idea' (such that his original title for the book was *Strategic Inflection Points,* until his publishers stepped in within the much more arresting *Only the Paranoid Survive*). In a business world that he characterizes as 'jungle law', SIPs are a vital tool in helping companies scan the horizon for seismic changes that can rewrite industry rules. SIPs are not limited to high-tech industries like Intel, but are particularly prevalent in that field.

The internet may just be the biggest SIP of all. Grove believes that within five years 'all companies will be internet companies or they won't be companies at all. In other words, companies not using the internet to improve just about every facet of their business operation will be destroyed by competitors who do.'

Zeitbite

Andy Grove on strategic inflection points

'An inflection point occurs where the old strategic picture dissolves and gives way to the new, allowing the business to ascend to new heights. So how do we know that a set of circumstances is a strategic inflection point?

'Most of the time, recognition takes place in stages:

'First, there is a troubling sense that something is different. Things don't work the way they used to. Customers' attitudes toward you are different. Competitors that you wrote off or hardly knew existed are stealing business from you.

'Then there is a growing dissonance between what your company thinks it is doing and what is actually happening inside the bowels of the organization. Such misalignment between corporate statements and operational actions hints at more than the normal chaos that you have learned to live with.

'Eventually, a new framework emerges. It's as if the group that was lost finds its bearings again. (This could take a year – or a decade.)

'Last of all, a new set of corporate statements is generated, often by a new set of senior managers.

'How do you know the right moment to take appropriate action, to make the changes that will save your company or your career? Unfortunately, you don't.

'But you can't wait until you do know: Timing is everything. If you undertake these changes while your company is still healthy, you can save much more of your company's strength, your employees and your strategic position. But that means acting when not everything is known, when the data aren't yet in. Even those who believe in a scientific approach to management will have to rely on instinct and personal judgement. When you're caught in the turbulence of a strategic inflection point, the sad fact is that instinct and judgement are all you've got to guide you through.

'But the good news is that even though your judgment got you into this tough position, it can also get you out. It's just a question of training your instincts to pick up a different set of signals. These signals may have been out there all along but you may have ignored them. The strategic inflection point is the time to wake up and listen.'

Taken and adapted from *Only the Paranoid Survive*

Although Grove is one of life's techno-determinists, it's becoming increasing difficult to quibble with this assessment. What is exciting and disquieting in equal measure is the thought that, as far as the internet is concerned, we are still in the hurricane's eye.

The author

Born in Hungary in 1936, Andy Grove emigrated to the US in 1956. After graduating with a PhD from the University of California at Berkeley, he joined the Fairchild Semiconductor Corp. before co-founding Intel in 1979. He stepped down as CEO of Intel in 1998, but continues as chairman of the board.

Sources and further reading

Andrew S Grove, 1996, *Only the Paranoid Survive: How to exploit the crisis points that challenge every company and career*, HarperCollins-Business, New York.

Tim Jackson, 1997, *Inside Intel*, HarperCollins, New York.
   A less flattering picture of Grove and Intel by a British journalist.

Michael Porter, 1980, *Competitive Strategy*, Free Press, New York.

GARY HAMEL & C K PRAHALAD,

Competing for the Future

1994

O ne of the ironies of conventional strategic analysis and planning is that it tends to orient us away from the big picture and into the detail. The big picture is something to be 'visited' periodically by the chosen few. The rest of the organization is supposed to implement 'bite-sized chunks' of the plan using action plans, milestones and short-term targets to allow progress to be monitored and measured. Normally, there are feedback loops built into the system to allow the organization to react to changes in the environment, but these processes tend to be cumbersome unless a real crisis threatens the very survival of the organization. The result is organizational sclerosis, and occasionally disaster.

In *Competing for the Future*, Gary Hamel & C K Prahalad question the traditional strategic approach and suggest that companies need to talk less of strategy and planning and think more about *strategizing*. To help companies achieve this paradigm shift, they offer a whole new vocabulary of strategy. They talk, for instance, of the importance of 'strategic intent', 'strategic architecture', 'industry foresight', and – probably the concept for which *Competing for the Future* is best known – 'core competencies'.

Hamel and Prahalad define core competencies as 'a bundle of skills and technologies (rather than a simple or discrete skill or technology) that enables the company to provide a particular benefit to customers'. They argue that companies gain benefit by thinking beyond their current product lines and being clear about and deploying effectively their underlying competencies. Applying this thinking reveals that a company such as Nike has a core competence of design and merchandising, not shoe quality. Sony pioneered transistor radios, but isn't still making them. Its core competency of miniaturization enables it to amaze consumers by pioneering new things to miniaturize. For McDonald's, convenience is a core competence.

For any organization, core competencies are necessarily limited in number. A company that believes itself to have 50 core competencies, for example, is probably describing constituent skills and technologies rather that core competencies. At the other extreme, a company that can list only one or two core competencies is likely to be using too broad a level of aggregation. Hamel and Prahalad take the view that, to be considered core, a competency must meet three tests:

1   *Customer value*: a core competency must make 'a disproportionate contribution to customer-perceived value'. They cite Honda's know-how in engines as a core competency, whereas its management of dealer relationships isn't. The fact is that very few of Honda's customers choose it over competitors because of some unique capability on the part of Honda's dealers; whereas their reputation for building some of the world's best engines does distinguish the company from the competition.
2   *Competitor differentiation*: a core competency must be competitively unique. This does not mean that it is uniquely held by just a single company, but it does mean that any capability that *is* ubiquitous in an industry sector is not a core competency.
3   *Extendibility*: core competencies rather than product lines are gateways to tomorrow's markets. Companies need to escape a product-centric view of their capabilities and be prepared to use their core competencies as a basis for entry into new product markets.

If a significant chunk of the power of core competencies rests in their capability to lever open new potential markets for a company, we should bear in mind that actually identifying those opportunities still requires a considerable act of corporate imagination. The trick is to see the future before it arrives. The industry foresight needed to achieve this, say Hamel and Prahalad, 'grows out of a childlike innocence about what could be and should be, out of a deep and boundless curiosity on the part of senior executives, and out of a willingness to speculate about issues where one is, as of yet, not an expert'.

If core competencies provide the potential for companies to move into new markets, and industry foresight enables those future markets to be imagined, that future still needs to be built. Hence Hamel and Prahalad's coining of the term 'strategic architecture'.

Building strategic architecture involves much more than 'rolling out' a long-term plan. It requires processes to be built that allow all the

Zeitbites

In *Competing for the Future*, Hamel and Prahalad offer up any number of pithy, insightful, thought-provoking and quotable sentences. Here are just a few examples:

- 'As a benchmark, our experience suggests that to develop a prescient and distinctive point of view about the future, a senior management team must be willing to spend about 20 to 50% of its time [building a corporate perspective on the future], over a period of several months.'
- 'Whole industries become vulnerable to new rules when all the incumbents accept, more or less, the same industry conventions.'
- 'Get your employees to feel a sense of urgency about the future, that they can make a difference. Avoid being hostage to existing markets. And develop foresight to create the future, not just in your company, but in your entire industry.'
- 'A company surrenders today's businesses when it gets smaller faster than it gets better. A company surrenders tomorrow's businesses when it gets better with getting different.'
- 'Markets mature, but competencies evolve.'
- 'Few companies understand how to leverage existing core competencies beyond the boundaries of current business units to create new competitive space.'
- 'Every company should ask itself where the opportunities are to broaden the deployment of existing competencies to strengthen position in existing markets.'
- 'Understanding industry structure is not the same thing as reshaping it.'

Taken from *Competing for the Future*

employees in the organization to see the big picture as well as their individual parts in making the future happen. To build new core competencies, the organization must have a holistic view of its relationship with its environment and the changes that are likely to occur in this relationship in future. Strategic architecture becomes the process which allows the organization to create an enlarged sense of future possibilities. But of course strategic architecture needs organizational architects.

Hamel and Prahalad describe an architect as both a dreamer and a draughtsman since the future requires both imagining and constructing. Organizations also need to build the processes to revisit the big picture continuously. To do this, they must recognize the value of all information, no matter where it is received within the organization. This 'top-to-bottom process' of challenging an organization's deepest assumptions about 'who we are and what we do' is fundamental to its success in the long term. This is the nature of organizations that truly create the future by changing the rules of the game rather than by playing within them.

Successful strategy is almost always an attempt to examine, and ultimately to go beyond, our current level of thinking. Hamel and Prahalad, as ever, put it succinctly: 'Much has been written about the need to manage tensions, trade-offs, paradoxes, and contradictions. Unfortunately much of this misses the point. The goal is not to find the narrow line between the unattractive extremes, nor to maintain an uneasy balance between counterposed forces. In short, the goal is not to occupy the middle ground; it is to find the higher ground.'

The authors

C K Prahalad is professor of business administration at the University of Michigan's Business School. He is a widely acknowledged guru of corporate strategy and has served as a consultant to several multinationals around the world. He is the author of several books on strategy and multinational management.

Gary Hamel is a professor of strategic and international management at the London Business School and chairman of the strategy consulting company, Strategos.

Sources and further reading

Gary Hamel and C K Prahalad, 1994, *Competing for the Future*, Harvard Business School Press, Boston.

Gary Hamel, 2000, *Leading the Revolution*, Harvard Business School Press, Boston.

Gary Hamel and C K Prahalad, July-August 1994, 'Competing for the Future', *Harvard Business Review*.

The main arguments of *Competing for the Future* are set out in this *HBR* article in which the authors question the traditional strategic approach and consider the critical importance of 'industry fore-sight' in determining organizational success.

Gary Hamel and C K Prahalad, May-June 1990, 'The Core Competence of the Corporation', *Harvard Business Review.*

Gary Hamel and C K Prahalad, May-June 1989, 'Strategic Intent', *Harvard Business Review.*

MICHAEL HAMMER & JAMES CHAMPY

Reengineering the Corporation

1993

T he successful implementation of any strategy requires that the internal or organizational architecture of the business is consistent and supportive. This can often require changing both organizational structure and processes to ensure that future customer needs can be anticipated and fulfilled in the most cost-effective manner. This exercise is generally known as business process redesign.

Mike Hammer, former MIT professor and widely regarded as the originator and prime driver behind the business reengineering movement, defines business process redesign as 'the fundamental rethinking and radical redesign of business processes to achieve dramatic improvements in critical, contemporary measures of performance'.

Process redesign should not be confused with crude cost-cutting exercises (such as downsizing), although many organizations have used both approaches simultaneously, with the result that the value of process redesign has been permanently tarnished in the eyes of many managers. Business process redesign has probably generated more negative press than any other management technique of the past decade.

Process redesign (commonly known as business process reengineering) is a management mongrel. On one side, its ancestors are Japanese theories about lean, flexible, just-in-time production, and on the other side, American ideas about redesigning companies from the bottom up. Since this may well mean a company having to rethink its processes and quite possibly start again from scratch, it can be an awesome task. However, it is important to recognize that process redesign should not be an aim in itself. It must be linked directly to the strategic objectives of the organization.

A business process exercise generally begins by looking critically at activities throughout the organization's value-added chain. Indeed, one of the advantages of a process-oriented approach is that it forces management (sometimes for the first time!) to identify the organization's value-added chain from the perspective of the customer. This is important because the way in which an organization meets or anticipates its customer needs is often a critical source of differentiation and competitive advantage. It emphasizes the need to change the nature of organizational design from meeting the needs of employees (who push products and services to the market) to meeting the needs of customers (who pull products and services through the organization).

Despite the many advantages of process redesign, it is not a panacea for organizational problems. It needs to be closely linked to:

- the strategic process: why streamline a business activity if technology is likely to render it obsolete? Managers need to reflect on what they are doing as well as how efficiently they are doing it;
- the alignment of technical factors and systems throughout the organization (for example reward and promotion incentives, etc.); and
- an awareness of organizational culture. The success of any change initiative depends ultimately on gaining the commitment of people in the organization.

Reengineering in general and Mike Hammer in particular faced much hostile criticism because the tool was used to justify an unprecedented bout of corporate bloodletting in the first half of the 1990s. Five years on from the publication of *Reengineering the Corporation*, Mike Hammer was interviewed by *Information Strategy* magazine about the bad press that business reengineering had picked up over the years. He gave his explanation:

> 'In the early nineties many companies were instinctively downsizing. They found it embarrassing to say so and they seized on reengineering as a euphemism to cover up a much more simplistic approach, of just throwing people out the window. What they were doing was not reengineering at all, but using the term as a more politically correct cloak to hide their real intentions. In the end, many people wound up thinking that reengineering and downsizing were the same thing.'

But, he argued later in the article, reengineering had also brought many benefits:

Reality check – small can be beautiful

'We must be careful not to equate successful change solely with dramatic transformation at the organizational level. Incremental improvement is also vital to the successful implementation of strategy. Most continuous improvement is bottom up, based on knowledge and depends on the existence of a culture in which people are empowered. It is usually incremental – move a filing cabinet, redesign a form, change the sequence of doing something, adapt an existing design, and so forth.

'It is easy to trivialize such change, to regard it as unimportant. However, this would be wrong. A powerful illustration of the power of continuous improvement is shown by the Japanese system of *kaizen*, which involves all employees in making improvements. The ideas tend to be small-scale, inexpensive to implement and concern the individual's own area of work. But the cumulative effect of these changes is impressive.'

From *Reengineering the Corporation*

'A lot of the massive corporate revenue growth we have seen in the last seven or eight years has been a direct consequence of the reengineering that was done. This didn't all come about merely through an increase in global demand. Nor were companies suddenly swimming in new customers they did not have before. What happened was that companies reduced cycle times on order fulfilment by 90%. They improved accuracy on invoices by 100%. They dramatically shortened product development times and really improved their operations by reengineering those processes.'

Reengineering was once described by *Fast Company* magazine as 'the fad that forgot people'. In truth, it has always been more popular with CEOs and their finance people than with the organization at large. There's no doubt that many companies, under the banner of reengineering, have cut a huge swathe through their workforces. In the UK alone, there were over four million redundancies between 1997 and 2002, most of them structural.

These days, reengineering has a lower profile but, according to Hammer, is more widely applied than ever. Having started out in the back office of large manufacturing companies, it has now moved into front office functions like sales, marketing and product development. In recent times, many service companies have applied it to improve their performance. Reengineering has been taken on board by smaller companies, and is also being applied across and between companies in improving supply chains.

The authors

Michael Hammer is generally credited with being the originator and leading exponent of the concept of business reengineering. He was named by *Business Week* magazine as one of the four pre-eminent management gurus of the 1990s.

James Champy is chairman of CSC Index and is a recognized authority on the implementation of business reengineering initiatives.

Sources and further reading

Michael Hammer and James Champy, 1993, *Reengineering the Corporation*, HarperCollins Publishers, New York.

Information Strategy, October 1998, features an interview with Hammer.

Daniel Pink, September 2001, 'Who has the next big idea?', *Fast Company*.
An interesting insight into what Hammer is thinking these days.

CHARLES HANDY
The Age of Unreason

1989

 any of the stories that appear in the media concern organizations facing transformational changes. Transformational change implies radical change caused by discontinuities, one-off changes, in the marketplace. Discontinuous change in the environment forces radical organizational change. Changes in key technologies, markets or the nature of competition are reflected in serious (sometimes life-threatening) declines in financial performance. There is often no doubt that the organization needs to transform itself to survive; the question is 'how?'

However, there is another, more common, form of change which is illustrated so well by Charles Handy in his book, *The Age of Unreason*. If you put a frog in water and slowly heat it, the frog will eventually let itself be boiled to death. This form of change, which is sometimes called strategic drift, happens incrementally and, often, imperceptibly. It is difficult to see because it is part of a larger system where cause and effect relationships are not obvious and where significant time lags are common. True, there will be warnings that all is not well, but these warnings are normally in the nature of anomalies or paradoxical circumstances, and as such can be easily dismissed. For example:

- increasingly negative customer feedback at the same time as rapid sales increases;
- increasing dependence on one product combined with healthy increases in both sales and margins;
- failure in one key market (for example, the US) combined with increasing market share in local regional markets (Europe).

All too often, organizations seek to explain anomalies as exceptions caused by a particular, but unrepresentative, set of factors. They seek to resolve the anomaly by pushing harder on levers that have been successful in the past. Unfortunately, this is often the very worst response because the 'exception' reflects a deeper level of reality that is not perceived by the organization. Hiring more salesmen, for example, will not be effective if basic customer needs have changed. Running ever-increasing budget deficits and increasing taxes to maintain the social minimum will not be effective for governments if globally oriented financial markets penalize them through higher interest rates. Where organizations fail to understand the larger systems at work, 'corrective' actions almost always make matters worse. Only by perceiving and addressing the *real* issues at stake can a vicious cycle be turned into a virtuous one.

In *The Age of Unreason*, Charles Handy tells a story to demonstrate the nature of discontinuous change: 'Thirty years ago I started work in a world-famous multinational company. By way of encouragement they produced an outline of my future career. "This will be your life", they said, "with titles of likely jobs". The line ended, I remember, with myself as Chief Executive of a particular company in a particular far-off country. I was, at the time, suitably flattered. I left them long before I reached the heights they planned for me, but I already knew that not only did the job they had picked out no longer exist, neither did the company I would have directed, nor even the country in which I was to have operated.'

This story nicely illustrates Handy's style – conversational, anecdotal and open. It also sums up what he means by 'the age of unreason': it's a time 'when the future, in so many areas, is to be shaped by us and for us; a time when the only prediction that will hold true is that no predictions will hold true; a time therefore for bold imaginings ... for thinking the unlikely and doing the unreasonable.'

Handy goes on to describe a number of organizational forms that will emerge in an age of unreason:

1 *The shamrock organization*: Handy describes this as 'a form of organization based around a core of essential executives and workers supported by outside contractors and part-time help'.
2 *The federal organization*: a form of decentralized set-up in which the centre's powers are given to it by the outlying groups; the centre therefore co-ordinates, advises, influences and suggests rather than directs or controls. Federalism, says Handy, is the way to combine the autonomy of individual parts with the economics of co-ordination.

Zeitbite

'It's obviously going to be a different kind of world in the next century ... It will be a world of fleas and elephants, of large conglomerates and small individual entities, of large political and economic blocs and small countries. The smart thing is to be the flea on the back of the elephant. Think of Ireland and the EU, or consultants and the BBC.

'A flea can be global as easily as one of the elephants but can more easily be swept away. Elephants are a guarantee of continuity but fleas provide the innovation. There will also be *ad hoc* organizations, temporary alliances of fleas and elephants to deliver a particular project.'

Charles Handy writing in the October 1999 edition of *CBI News*

3 *The Triple I organization*: the three 'Is' are Information, Intelligence and Ideas. Handy says that this type of organization will resemble a university and will seek to make 'added value out of knowledge'. To achieve this end, this type of organization 'increasingly uses smart machines, with smart people to work with them'.

Not only was Handy remarkably prescient in anticipating the growth of outsourcing, telecommuting, the intellectual capital movement, the rise of knowledge workers, and several other developments, he also foresaw how they might impact on the individual. It was his concept of the portfolio worker that arguably provided a way forward for that part of the whole downshifting movement of the nineties that was wrestling with redefining the nature of work as well as questions of life balance.

The Age of Unreason reveals Handy at the peak of his powers as a management thinker. In later books and articles, he increasingly assumed the mantle of a social philosopher.

The author

Charles Handy is a writer, lecturer, broadcaster, and self-styled social philosopher. He divides his time between living and working in London and his rural retreat in Norfolk.

Sources and further reading

Charles Handy, 1989, *The Age of Unreason*, Hutchinson, London.

Charles Handy, 1999, *The New Alchemists*, Hutchinson, London.
This book features a series of interviews with 29 people who have made something out of nothing in either the business or arts worlds, or for the community. Those featured include inventor Trevor Baylis (creator of the clockwork radio), Andy Law of the St Luke's advertising agency, Geoff Mulgan (founder of Demos), Tim Waterstone of the eponymous bookshop, BA's Bob Ayling (whose inclusion seems open to question, to be honest) and the UK's master alchemist Richard Branson. And what makes an alchemist? According to Handy, they have three over-riding qualities:
- *dedication*: caring passionately about what they are trying to bring into being;
- *doggedness*: a wholehearted commitment to achieving results through hard work, determination and tenacity; and
- *difference*: a mixture of personality and talent that leads alchemists to do things differently or to do different things.

Charles Handy, 1997, *The Hungry Spirit*, Hutchinson, London.
The Hungry Spirit sees Handy drawing together his business and spiritual interests as he looks at how the rawer aspects of capitalism can co-exist with the search for an inner meaning to life. Different readers will form different conclusions about *The Hungry Spirit*. Those who share Handy's quest for meaning in work and life will find much to applaud; more pragmatic readers in search of new business ideas may feel short-changed.

Charles Handy, 1994, *The Empty Raincoat*, Hutchinson, London.
Contains some useful expansion of Handy's ideas about federal organizations.

Charles Handy, 1994, *Understanding Organizations* (4th edition), Penguin, London.

PAUL HAWKEN, AMORY B LOVINS & L HUNTER LOVINS

Natural Capitalism

1999

G enuinely original and insightful books are hard to find. So a book that claims that it portrays opportunities that, if captured, will lead to no less than a transformation of commerce and all societal institutions deserves a closer look.

The authors put forward a new approach for reconciling ecological and economic priorities, one that not only protects the earth's environment but also improves profits and competitiveness. 'Not possible' is our first, and quite natural, response because we have been taught that environmental and economic priorities are contradictory.

The authors argue otherwise, that the best solutions are based on design integration at all levels of economic activity. This principle recognizes not only human, financial and manufactured capital but also natural capital; the resources, living systems and ecosystem services of our world. They call this approach 'natural capitalism'.

The book outlines four central strategies of natural capitalism, which are interrelated and interdependent. All four offer numerous benefits and opportunities in markets, finance, materials, distribution and employment:

1 *Radical resource productivity.* This is the cornerstone of natural capitalism. Fundamental changes in both production design and technology offer us the opportunity to develop ways to make natural resources – energy, minerals, water, forests – stretch five, ten, even a hundred times further than they do today.
2 *A shift to biologically inspired production models.* Bio-mimicry seeks not only to reduce waste but to eliminate the very concept of waste. In closed-loop production systems, modelled on nature's designs, every output is returned harmlessly to the ecosystem as a nutri-

Zeitbite

Natural capitalism as win-win

'At its simplest, increasing resource productivity means obtaining the same amount of utility or work from a product or process while using less material or energy. In manufacturing, transportation, forestry, construction, energy, and other industrial sectors, mounting empirical evidence suggests that radical improvements in resource productivity are both practical and cost-effective, even in the most modern industries. Companies and designers are developing ways to make natural resources – energy, metals, waters and forests – work five, ten, even one hundred times harder than they do today. These efficiencies transcend the marginal gains in performance that industry constantly seeks as part of its evolution. Instead, revolutionary leaps in design and technology will alter industry itself.'

Taken from *Natural Capitalism*

ent, like compost, or becomes an input for manufacturing another product.

3 *A move to a solutions-based business model.* The business model of traditional manufacturing rests on the sale of goods. In the new model, value is instead delivered as a flow of services, which reduces consumption but improves consumer choice (for example, access to the entire music catalogues of music companies by subscription rather than purchasing individual CDs).

4 *Reinvesting in natural capital.* Sustaining, restoring and expanding natural stocks of capital to work towards reversing world-wide planetary destruction.

Accustomed as we are to so many business books promising us the moon, it is only natural that we become somewhat cynical and jaded. *Natural Capitalism* is different. This book delivers.

The authors

Paul Hawken is an environmentalist, educator and best-selling author. He has served on the board of several organizations, including Conservation International, Friends of the Earth, and the National Audubon

Society. He received the 1999 Green Cross Millennium Award for International Environmental Leadership.

Amory B Lovins and L Hunter Lovins are co-chief executive officers of the Rocky Mountain Institute in Colorado, which they founded in 1982.

Consultants to several companies worldwide, they are co-authors (with Ernst von Weizsäcker) of the best-selling *Factor Four: Doubling Wealth, Halving Resource Use*. Ernst von Weizsäcker is president of the Wuppertal Institute for Climate, Environment and Energy in the North-Rhine/Westphalian Science Centre, Germany. He was previously professor of biology at Essen University. In 1996, he was the first recipient of the Duke of Edinburgh Gold Medal of WWF International.

Sources and further reading

Paul Hawken, Amory B Lovins, and L Hunter Lovins, 1999, *Natural Capitalism: The next industrial revolution*, Earthscan Publications Ltd, London.

Ernst von Weizsäcker, Amory B Lovins, and L Hunter Lovins, 1997, *Factor Four: Doubling Wealth, Halving Resource Use*, Earthscan Publications Ltd, London.

First a definition of Factor Four: 'Factor Four, in a nutshell, means that resource productivity can and should grow fourfold. The amount of wealth extracted from one unit of natural resources can quadruple. Thus we can live twice as well yet use half as much.'

The practical promise held out in this book is huge, although it is up to businesses and governments, as well as each of us individually, to take it. Although not the easiest of reads, *Factor Four* does seem to be getting into the hands of political and social agenda-setters. It may prove to be a highly influential book, and certainly its underlying philosophy ought to appeal to the heads and pockets of the business community.

The publisher of both books has a useful website which can be found at www.earthscan.co.uk

ROBERT KAPLAN & DAVID NORTON

The Balanced Scorecard

1996

A s we know, the last ten years have witnessed dramatic changes in performance measurement, resulting from the increasingly sophisticated use of IT, flaws in conventional management accounting techniques, and for many companies the integration of financial performance measures into the strategic management system as a whole.

The most important innovation in the field of performance measurement in recent times has been the balanced scorecard, a strategic management system developed by Robert Kaplan and David Norton of the Harvard Business School. The balanced scorecard is designed to enable companies to track financial results while simultaneously monitoring progress in building the capabilities and acquiring the intangible assets they need for future growth.

The Balanced Scorecard is a seminal work. Many management writers have written in general terms on the limitations of relying on traditional financial measures to assess business performance. But few have set out specifically with the aim of building a comprehensive framework of broadly based performance measures that provides a process for organizations to link long-term strategic objectives with short-term actions. By doing precisely this, Kaplan and Norton have managed to place performance measurement at the heart of long-term organizational success.

In *The Balanced Scorecard*, the authors demonstrate how to use measures in four categories – financial performance, customer knowledge, internal business processes, and learning and growth – to build a robust learning system that aligns individual, organizational, and cross-departmental initiatives in building long-term strategic advantage. Here are some typical measures that might be deployed under each of the four categories.

Financial perspective
- Return on Capital – ROCE
- Return on Sales – ROS
- Revenue per employee
- Project profitability
- Break-even analysis
- Cash flow/payback

Customer perspective
- Market share
- Customer retention
- Customer acquisition
- Customer satisfaction
- Customer profitability

Internal business perspective
- Rate of innovation
- Post-sale service
- Operational efficiency
- Measures of quality, yield, throughput and cycle time

Innovation and learning perspective
- Employee satisfaction
- Employee retention
- Employee productivity
- Information system capabilities
- Other system 'enablers'.

Kaplan and Norton go on to show how any organization can use its own particular mix of these measures to build a consensus around the organization's strategy, and then go on to communicate and link strategy to individual and unit goals. Perhaps most important of all, an organization can build the capacity for strategic learning by gathering feedback and testing the hypotheses on which the strategy was based.

In fact, one of the major strengths of the balanced scorecard is that it allows strategy to evolve in response to changes in the markets and the competitive environment of the organization.

Over the eight years or so since Kaplan and Norton formulated the concept of the balanced scorecard, it has been adopted by literally thou-

> **Zeitbite**
>
> 'As companies around the world transform themselves for competition that is based on information, their ability to exploit intangible assets has become far more decisive than their ability to invest in and manage physical assets.'
>
> Taken from 'Using a Balanced Scorecard as a Strategic Management System'.

sands of organizations as the cornerstone of their strategic management systems, driving the implementation of strategy by linking performance measures directly to the overall vision of the business and key strategic objectives.

This link is achieved by asking four key questions for each of the four main areas of performance criteria:

1 What is our vision of the future? *which leads to:*
2 If our vision succeeds how will the organization differ? *which leads to:*
3 What are the critical success factors? *which leads to:*
4 What are the critical measurements?

Kaplan and Norton argue that effective measurement must be an integral part of the management process. The real value of the balanced scorecard is that it provides executives with a comprehensive framework that translates a company's strategic objectives into a coherent set of performance measures. Much more than a management exercise, the balanced scorecard is a management system that can motivate breakthrough improvements in such critical areas as product, process, customer and market development. All of which makes Kaplan and Norton's book a must-read for all senior organizational players who believe in building for the long term.

The authors

Robert Kaplan is the Marvin Bower Professor of Leadership Development at Harvard Business School. He joined the HBS faculty in 1984.

David Norton is the president of Renaissance Solutions Inc.

Sources and further reading

Robert S Kaplan and David P Norton, 1996, *The Balanced Scorecard*, Harvard Business School, Boston.

Robert S Kaplan and David P Norton, 2001, *The Strategy Focused Organization*, Harvard Business School, Boston.

Robert S Kaplan and David P Norton, January/February 1996, 'Using a Balanced Scorecard as a Strategic Management System', *Harvard Business Review.*

JOHN KAY

Foundations of Corporate Success

1993

O rganizations succeed in the marketplace if they add value in the eyes of their customers. As a result, value-added is a key concept in strategy and a critical measurement of competitive advantage.

John Kay puts it succinctly: 'Adding value is the central purpose of business activity. A commercial organization that adds no value – whose output is worth no more than the value of its inputs in alternative uses – has no long-term rationale for its existence.'

It might be useful to define the term. Value-added is, crudely, the difference between the value of a firm's output and the cost of the firm's inputs. Technically, it is the difference between the market value of output and the cost of inputs including the cost of capital (it is the latter which differentiates a value-added statement from a profit or loss statement). It can also be expressed as a ratio (value added as a proportion of a firm's net or gross output). The fundamental premise underlying value chain analysis is adding maximum value at minimum cost. In all organizations, costs (relative to benefits!) should decrease over time.

In practice, however, measurement of value-added is difficult because of the many invisible/psychological attributes of products or services. For example, value can be 'objective' or 'perceived', although in truth it should always be assessed from the point of view of the final customer or user of the product or service. Also, many of the measures of added value are relative rather than absolute (hence the importance of 'benchmarking' and establishing 'best practice').

Adding value then is the target for every organization, particularly those with a commercial purpose. How to add value is another matter. For just as each of us is unique, so is every organization.

For this reason alone, the tools and techniques that an organization needs to deploy in its quest to add value will differ according to a number of factors, including the size of the organization, its markets, its industry, and its environment. Moreover, the choice of tools and techniques needs to be timely; for example, a customer survey designed at the beginning of a relationship may not be appropriate at a later date when the customer has grown in size and importance to the business.

Unfortunately, there is no easy process to determine which tools and techniques to use at any one point of time. If it were any other way, strategy would be easy! As John Kay remarks, 'There are no recipes [or] generic strategies for corporate success. There cannot be, because if there were their general adoption would eliminate any competitive advantage which might be derived. The foundations of corporate success are unique to each successful company.'

In his book, Kay sets out his thinking about what these foundations of corporate success might be. He argues that the answer lies in two key areas:

1   *external positioning*: the relationship between the organization and the external world in terms of its markets, customers and the broader environment (what's going on around it); and

2   *internal capabilities or competencies*: (what the organization is good at). Companies with distinctive capabilities have attributes which others cannot replicate, even after they realize the benefit they offer to the company which originally possesses them. Kay refers to these distinctive capabilities as 'something an organization can do that its potential competitors cannot … based on its unique set of relationships in the marketplace'.

Business strategy, according to Kay, involves identifying a firm's distinctive capabilities: putting together a collection of complementary assets and capabilities, and maximizing and defending the economic benefits which result.

According to Kay, a company's distinctive capabilities are potentially located in one or more of the three following areas:

1   *Architecture*: a system of relationships within an organization, or between an organization and its employees, suppliers and customers or all of them. 'The value of architecture', Kay writes, 'rests in the capacity of organizations which establish it to create organizational knowledge and routine, to respond flexibly to changing circumstances, and to achieve easy and open exchanges of informa-

---

Strategy defined by John Kay

'Competitive strategy is concerned with the firm's position relative to its competitors in the markets which it has chosen. The strategy of the firm is the match between its internal capabilities and its external relationships.'

Taken from *Foundations of Corporate Success*

---

tion.' Architecture is about establishing and maintaining the right environment, the right culture, rather than simply buying in talent. As Kay puts it, 'Architecture does not create extraordinary organizations by collecting extraordinary people. It does so by enabling very ordinary people to perform in extraordinary ways'.

2 *Reputation*: the most important commercial mechanism for conveying information to consumers. Reputation is often closely linked to the brands that a company owns and manages. Although not equally important in all markets, when it is important, loss of reputation can be devastating, as Andersen's spectacular fall from grace on the back of the Enron scandal has shown. Reputation is, paradoxically, both the easiest to sustain and the most fragile of the distinctive capabilities.

3 *Innovation*: the change or improvement in the products or services of an organization or the process by which they are produced. The process of innovation often involves complex interactions between companies. Kay explores two common innovation processes, the first in which one innovator can scoop the pool by, for example, winning a patent race, and the second process in which success depends on the establishment of common technical standards.

A fourth source of competitive advantage derives not from the distinctive capabilities of a company but rather from the extent to which it dominates its chosen markets.

These 'Strategic Assets' fall into three main categories:

1 *natural monopoly*: where a company is already established in a market that does not readily accommodate more than one presence;

2 *cost structure*: where incumbent companies have already incurred many of the costs of supply, thus giving them an advantage over new entrants who have not; and

3 *market restrictions*: where companies benefit from regulatory frameworks or from holding licences.

Kay believes that all of these sources of market advantage, whether they
are distinctive capabilities or strategic assets, are easier to hold onto
than they are to acquire. He warns, though, that distinctive capabilities
continue to add value only if both the capability and the distinctiveness
are sustainable. Also, a source of competitive advantage must be appro-
priable (appropriability is defined by Kay as 'the capacity of the firm to
retain the added value it creates for its own benefit').

John Kay's achievement in *Foundations of Corporate Success* is
immense. Drawing on a mixture of his own business experience and
concepts in economics, legal theory and sociology, he has brought a
fresh and convincing approach to questions of business strategy. Given
the book's age, perhaps it isn't surprising that some of the case studies he
uses – Liverpool Football Club, Marks & Spencer, and so on – have lost
some of their lustre. Despite this, his central thesis has held up remarkably well over the past ten years, and so an updated edition would be
very welcome.

The author

John Kay is one of Britain's leading economists. As well as a distinguished academic career including stints at the London Business School
and the University of Oxford, he built a successful consultancy called
London Economics. Following a serious illness in 1999, he sold his stake
in his consultancy and set aside his academic commitments to concentrate on reading, reflection and writing.

Sources and further reading

John Kay, 1993, *Foundations of Corporate Success*, Oxford Press,
Oxford.

John Kay has his own website, which is a useful source of information, and
contains a number of articles that he has written (www.johnkay.com).
He is currently working on a book entitled *How Markets Work*, due to be
published by Allen Lane in May 2003.

New Rules for the New Economy

I f the new economy needed to elect a founding father, Kevin Kelly would be on most people's list of nominations. As the first editor of *Wired* magazine in the early 1990s, Kevin Kelly quickly built a reputation as one of the new economy's creators and biographers.

In *New Rules for the New Economy*, Kelly sets out to identify the underlying principles that govern how the wired world operates. His starting point is that ideas and assumptions about the nature of work and the operating patterns of organizations that stem from the Age of the Machine simply don't make sense in the revolutionary Age of the Network. Success, maintains Kelly, flows primarily from understanding networks – how they behave, and the rules that govern them.

At the heart of the network revolution is communication. Kelly writes that communication is the foundation of society, of our culture, of our humanity, of our own individual identity, and of all economic systems. This is why networks are such a big deal. Communication is so close to culture and society itself that the effects of technologizing it are beyond the scale of a mere industrial-sector cycle. Communication, and its ally computers, is a special case in economic history. Not because it happens to be the fashionable leading business sector of our day, but because its cultural, technological and conceptual impacts reverberate at the root of our lives.

New Rules for the New Economy takes the form of ten 'rules', each given a chapter in the book. Kelly formulated these guiding principles by asking some fundamental questions. How do our tools shape our destiny? What kind of economy is our new technology suggesting? What became clear to him was, he writes, that 'steel ingots and rivers of oil, smokestacks and factory lines, and even tiny seeds and cud-chewing

Zeitbite

Kevin Kelly's 10 New Rules for the New Economy

1 *Embrace the swarm*: as power flows away from the centre, the competitive advantage belongs to those who learn how to embrace decentralized points of control.

2 *Increasing returns*: as the number of connections between people and things add up, the consequences of those connections multiply out even faster, so that initial successes aren't self-limiting, but self-feeding.

3 *Plentitude, not scarcity*: as manufacturing techniques perfect the art of making copies plentiful, value is carried by abundance, rather than scarcity, inverting traditional business propositions.

4 *Follow the free*: as resource scarcity gives way to abundance, generosity begets wealth. Following the free rehearses the inevitable fall of prices, and takes advantage of the only true scarcity: human attention.

5 *Feed the web first*: as networks entangle all commerce, a firm's primary focus shifts from maximizing the firm's value to maximizing the network's value. Unless the net survives, the firm perishes.

6 *Let go at the top*: as innovation accelerates, abandoning the highly successful in order to escape from its eventual obsolescence becomes the most difficult and yet most essential task.

7 *From places to spaces*: as physical proximity (place) is replaced by multiple interactions with anything, anytime, anywhere (space), the opportunities for intermediaries, middlemen, and mid-size niches expand greatly.

8 *No harmony, all flux*: as turbulence and instability become the norm in business, the most effective survival stance is a constant but highly selective disruption that we call innovation.

9 *Relationship technology*: as the soft trumps the hard, the most powerful technologies are those that enhance, amplify, extend, augment, distil, recall, expand, and develop soft relationships of all types.

10 *Opportunities before efficiencies*: as fortunes are made by training machines to be ever more efficient, there is yet far greater wealth to be had by unleashing the inefficient discovery and creation of new opportunities.

Derived from *New Rules for the New Economy*

cows are all becoming enmeshed in the world of smart chips and fast bandwidth, and sooner or later they will begin to fully obey the new rules'.

The ten rules themselves are a pithy guide to business survival in the internet age. But don't let the brevity of the book fool you – there is no evidence that Kelly has skimped on his thinking. In fact, one of his real talents is an ability to absorb and synthesize large amounts of information (his first book, *Out of Control*, came with a 300-title annotated bibliography at the back).

A definition of genius is the ability to look at the same world as everybody else and draw different conclusions. It's an ability that Kelly clearly has in abundance. Beyond that, as this lucid and awe-inspiring book shows, he is equally capable of reporting back what he sees. File under 'New Economy Classic'.

The author

Born in Pennsylvania and brought up in New Jersey, Kevin Kelly dropped out of college to spend eight years trekking around India, Nepal, and the Far and Middle East. On his return to the US, Kelly began to discover the on-line world, and through this he developed contacts that led to him landing a job as editor of *Whole Earth Review*, before going on to became founding editor at *Wired*. He left the role when the magazine was sold, but remains an editor-at-large. He is reported to be working on a project to list all the 30 million or so species of life on earth.

Sources and further reading

Kevin Kelly, 1998, *New Rules for the New Economy: 10 ways the network economy is changing everything*, Fourth Estate, London.

Kevin Kelly, 1994, *Out of Control: The new biology of machines*, Addison Wesley Inc, New York.

Kelly has a website at www.well.com/user/kk/, and the full text of *Out of Control* can be found at www.well.com/user/kk/OutOfControl/

Andrew Davidson's article 'The Net Prophet', *Financial Times*, 3 June 2000, is a highly readable and informative article about Kelly.

NICOLÓ MACHIAVELLI

The Prince

1513

bout 20 years ago, there was a marvellous episode of the BBC political comedy series *Yes Minister* called *The Moral Dimension*. In it, British government minister Jim Hacker and a delegation of civil servants are travelling to Qumran, an oil-rich Islamic country, to seal an export order. Alarmed to learn that no alcohol will be served at an upcoming reception, Hacker suggests setting up a 'communications room' stocked with alcohol brought in from the British Embassy. During the reception, Hacker is presented with a gift from the Qumran government: a valuable seventeenth century rosewater jar. His wife really likes the jar, but a civil servant, Bernard, explains to her that the minister is not allowed to keep this gift if it is worth more than £50. Meanwhile, Hacker is getting regular messages that he is needed in the communications room to deal with a Mr Haig, Mr Johnnie Walker, Mr Smirnoff, a group of Teachers, and so on.

Bernard talks with a Qumrani official who overheard the conversation he had with Hacker's wife, and offers to help in valuing the rosewater jar, falsely declaring it a copy and worth just under £50. Back in England, a journalist friend of the minister's wife is interested in the rosewater jar. The journalist decides to check out the value with the Qumrani Embassy.

When Hacker learns about the rosewater jar story, he is outraged that Bernard could have put him in this position. The journalist is outside demanding to see the minister, and Hacker announces he will tell the truth, citing 'the moral dimension'. Senior civil servant Sir Humphrey agrees fully that there is a moral dimension. He asks whether Jim Hacker will tell the press about Jim's idea for a communications room in Qumran or shall he? Hacker has no choice: he must either confess everything or deny everything. In a bravura performance, he denies everything.

If Nicoló Machiavelli had inhabited 1980s England rather than sixteenth-century Italy, one suspects he would have been amused by, and could even have scripted this *Yes Minister* episode. He would certainly have recognized a political world driven more by resolute pragmatism than morality, for that is a world he describes at length in *The Prince*.

That his book is still in print 500 years after it was written reflects the timelessness of its content. Its main theme, that princes should retain absolute control of their territories, and they should use any means of expediency to accomplish this end, as well as many of his practical insights into the nature of leadership and strategy, would get a hearty nod of approval from a certain breed of today's senior managers.

Machiavelli's most famous work was not published until 1532, five years after his death. The book provoked almost immediate controversy and was condemned by Pope Clement VIII as immoral. Scholars of the time were sharply divided in their interpretation of Machiavelli's precise point. Some took his words at face value while others saw *The Prince* as a satire on rulers such as the Borgias, who were infamous for their displays of arbitrary power. However, in 1810, a letter by Machiavelli was discovered in which he revealed that he wrote *The Prince* as part of a serious effort to endear himself to the ruling Medici family in Florence.

Over the years, Machiavelli's extremely pragmatic view of the relationship between ethics and politics has been widely misinterpreted. His surname, of course, has generated an adjective that is a byword for people who prefer expediency to morality, and who manipulate others in an opportunistic and deceptive way. This isn't altogether fair on Machiavelli: yes, he advocated deploying the darker side of human nature to achieve the desired goals, but only when, as he put it, 'necessity commands'.

Machiavelli's messages for managers

The most controversial aspects of Machiavelli's analysis emerge in the middle chapters of his work. Here are some of his key points:

- Machiavelli describes those virtues which a prince should possess. He concludes that some 'virtues' will lead to a prince's destruction, whereas some 'vices' allow him to survive. Indeed, the virtues which we commonly praise in people might lead to his downfall.

Machiavellian Zeitbites

'No enterprise is more likely to succeed than one concealed from the enemy until it is ripe for execution.'

'There is nothing more difficult to take in hand, more perilous to conduct, or more uncertain in its success, than to take the lead in the introduction of a new order of things.'

'As a prince must be able to act just like a beast, he should learn from the fox and the lion; because the lion does not defend himself against traps, and the fox does not defend himself against wolves. So one has to be a fox in order to recognize traps, and a lion to frighten off wolves.'

Taken from *The Prince*

(Chapter 15: *Concerning things for which men, and especially princes, are praised or blamed.*)

- Although we might think that it is best for a prince to have a reputation of being generous, Machiavelli writes that 'liberality exercised in a way that does not bring you the reputation for it, injures you.' On the other hand, if liberality is done openly, then a prince risks going broke to maintain his reputation. This will lead him to extort more money from his subjects and as a result come to be hated. Machiavelli's solution? It is wiser, he writes, to have a reputation for meanness, because that brings 'reproach without hatred'. (Chapter 16: *Concerning liberality and meanness.*)
- He argues that it is better for a prince to be severe when punishing people rather than merciful. Severity through death sentences affects only a few, but it deters crimes which affects many. Further, he argues, it is better to be feared than to be loved. (Chapter 17: *Concerning cruelty and clemency.*)
- In perhaps the most controversial section of *The Prince*, Machiavelli argues that a prince should know how to be deceitful when it suits his purpose. When the prince needs to be deceitful, though, he must not appear that way. Indeed he must always exhibit five virtues in particular: mercy, honesty, humaneness, uprightness, and religiousness. (Chapter 18: *Concerning the ways in which princes should keep faith.*)
- Machiavelli argues that the prince must avoid doing things which will cause him to be hated. This is accomplished by not confiscating property, and not appearing greedy or wishy-washy. In fact, the

best way to avoid being overthrown is to avoid being hated. (Chapter 19: *That one should avoid being despised and hated.*)

The author

Nicoló Machiavelli was born in Florence in 1469 and served as an official in the Florentine government. He had a successful and influential career until 1512, when the Medici family regained power with the help of Spanish troops. He was tortured and removed from public life, and for the next ten years he devoted himself to writing history, political philosophy, and plays. In 1525, he regained favour with the Medici family and was called back to public duty for the last two years of his life before dying in 1527.

Sources and further reading

Nicoló Machiavelli, *The Prince*, Everyman's Library, London, 1908; several other published versions are available.

T here's a Marx Brothers' film – *A Night in Casablanca* – in which Groucho Marx is hired to run a hotel whose previous managers have all wound up being murdered. Shortly after arriving, he makes an announcement to the staff, which goes along the lines of: 'There are going to have to be some changes around here: from now on, if a guest asks for a three-minute egg, give him a two-minute egg; if he asks for a two-minute egg, give him a one-minute egg; and if he asks for a one-minute egg, give him the chicken and tell him to work it out for himself.'

Although in that case Groucho's motives were more profit- than customer-driven, most modern-day managers know that we are living in an age of ever more demanding customers. They want better quality, they want cheaper prices and, above all, they want it now. The bookshop owner who tells customers that it will take two weeks to order in the book they want is seeing increasing volumes of business going to internet sites like Amazon. Until quite recently, you had physically to go to a bank to get a balance on your account; now it's available on-line, more or less instantly.

Providing an immediate, customer-satisfying response to any request is a tough challenge for any business. But, says Regis McKenna, any company that wishes to remain in the marketplace has only one choice – it must become a real-time business.

How are companies to achieve this transformation? Having great technology will help to compress time, says McKenna, but just as critically companies must challenge conventional wisdom about how they operate. Traditional facets of company life – hierarchy, long-term planning methodologies – need to go, to be replaced by 'real-time managers' who focus on delivery and results, and who recognize that customized service is the new corporate mantra. Getting more specific, McKenna goes on to provide examples and ideas from companies that have gained a practical understanding of how time, technology and customer service are interrelated.

The book's contents are neatly summed up at regular intervals by a number of what McKenna calls 'real-time messages'. To give a flavour, here are a few examples:

- On creating the real-time company: 'The task of implementing a real-time corporation is difficult and complex, but it is an essential investment in your competitive future. The implementation of real-time systems will have the effect of changing the working relationships within your organization as well as those with your partners and customers. The application of the technology will change your corporate culture. As these systems are adopted, new ideas for services and products, new ways of gaining customer loyalty, and new methods of team collaboration will take shape. Then information technology will indeed become a valued corporate asset.'

- On satisfying the never-satisfied customer: 'New consumers are never satisfied consumers. Managers hoping to serve them must work to eliminate time and space constraints on service. They must push the technological bandwidth with interactive dialogue systems – equipped with advanced software interfaces – in the interest of forging more intimate ties with these consumers. Managers must exploit every available means to obtain their end: building self-satisfaction capabilities into services and products and providing customers with access anytime, anywhere.'

- On being prepared for anything: 'Companies will learn about the technologies of real time in the only way they truly can – by adopting them and putting them to practical use. They will deploy them not to predict the future but to live virtually on top of changing patterns and trends affecting every sphere of their business environment, making rapid and continuous refinements in their way of doing business.'

When *Real Time* was first published, it received excellent reviews in America, and a number of well-respected CEOs – including Fred Smith of Federal Express and HP's Lew Platt – sang its praises ('McKenna's insights will excite and shock you', said Platt). Although the messages of the book seem far less radical now than five years ago, McKenna's analysis remains just as valid, as does his emphasis on customized service and time-based competition. Companies that turn away from McKenna's

> **Zeitbite**
>
> 'Winning organizations will be run in the expectation of relentless shifts and readjustments in the marketplace, in customers' expectations, and in the behaviour of competitors. Like Lewis Carroll's Queen, they will anticipate surprises six times a day before breakfast.'
>
> Regis McKenna

prescription may well come in time to face the corporate significance of another of Groucho's lines – 'I've had a wonderful evening, but this wasn't it.'

The author

Regis McKenna is chairman of The McKenna Group, based in Palo Alto, California. He regularly lectures and conducts seminars on technology marketing and competitiveness. McKenna is the author of three other books – *The Regis Touch, Who's afraid of Big Blue?* and *Relationship Marketing.*

Sources and further reading

Regis McKenna, 1997, *Real time: preparing for the age of the never-satisfied customer*, Harvard Business School Press, Boston.

McKenna's company website can be found at www.mckenna-group.com

HENRY MINTZBERG

The Rise and Fall of Strategic Planning

1994

pparently, there's a sign on the door of actor Paul Newman's work office which reads: 'If we ever have a plan, we're screwed'.

I suspect that Henry Mintzberg would thoroughly approve of Newman's sentiments. Perhaps more than any of the big names in the strategy field, Mintzberg has undermined our perception of strategy as a 'hard' discipline with its roots in planning and analysis. He suggests instead that the future is to all intents unknowable and that the discipline of strategic planning needs to absorb the implications of this.

In 'Crafting Strategy', one of the best-known articles on strategy to appear in the *Harvard Business Review* in the last 20 years, Mintzberg uses the analogy of the potter's wheel to liken the strategic process to a craft. He argues that strategies need not necessarily be deliberate but can also emerge through circumstances, that it can *form* rather than need to be *formulated*. While strategy is a word that is usually associated with the future, its link to the past is no less central. Like potters at the wheel, organizations must make sense of the past if they hope to manage the future. Only by coming to understand the patterns that form in their own behaviour do they get to know their capabilities and their potential.

Strategy, says Mintzberg, provides a means by which organizations and individuals can examine their internal and external worlds. As the business world has lost confidence in the traditional strategic perspective that the future is predictable, relatively slow to unfold and therefore readily manageable, gone is any sense that there is a 'one best way' to 'do' strategy.

In his 1994 classic *The Rise and Fall of Strategic Planning*, Mintzberg traces the origins and history of strategic planning through its prominence and subsequent fall, and sets out what he sees as some of the fundamental fallacies of strategic planning, for example that discontinuities can be predicted, that strategists can be detached from the operations of the organization, and that the process of strategy-making itself can be formalized.

Thus we arrive at what Mintzberg terms the planning school's grand fallacy: because analysis is not synthesis, strategic planning is not strategy formation. That is why, he asserts, the process has failed so often and so dramatically. As he puts it, 'The whole nature of strategy making – dynamic, irregular, discontinuous, calling for groping, interactive processes with an emphasis on learning and synthesis – compels managers to favour intuition. This is probably why all those analytical techniques of planning felt so wrong. ... Ultimately, the term "strategic planning" has proved to be an oxymoron.'

It shouldn't be inferred from this that Mintzberg believes that detailed analysis is no longer necessary in the strategic process. There will always be a need for an objective evaluation process that ensures that the organization has been through a logical sequence of steps designed to think through the ramifications of a decision. But the primary purpose of this process, says Mintzberg, should be to probe and challenge assumptions, surface mental models or mind-sets that are shared by those in the decision-making process, and to ask the 'what if' and 'why not' questions that extend the boundaries of organizational awareness.

For Mintzberg, the most compelling and convincing strategic processes are those that are capable of synthesizing a vision. This being so, Mintzberg would easily relate to how Mozart once described the act of composing: 'First bits and crumbs of the piece come and gradually join together in my mind; then the soul getting warmed to the work, the thing grows more and more, and I spread it out broader and clearer, and at last it gets almost finished in my head, even when it is a long piece, so that I can see the whole of it at a single glance in my mind, as if it were a beautiful painting or a handsome human being; in which way I do not hear it in my imagination at all as a succession – the way it must come later – but all at once as it were. It is a rare feast. All the inventing and making goes on in me as in a beautiful strong dream. But the best of all is the hearing of it all at once.'

Mintzberg is one of life's heretics, and what he has to say is radically different from most other writers on strategy. He is a fierce challenger of conventional wisdom. What irks many of his critics is that he is generally proved right. As Rod White, a business professor at the University of Western Ontario, has put it, 'Henry is always prepared to go straight into the lion's den. And the lions usually lose.'

Zeitbite

'Peters and Waterman ... made famous the "Ready. Fire. Aim." comment of a Cadbury's executive. In fact, this makes a great deal of sense, as long as one gets to fire more than once, which is normally the case. Extend the phrase and you have strategy formation as a learning process: "Ready-fire-aim-fire-aim-fire-aim," etc. Just as structure must always follow strategy, the way the left foot must follow the right foot walking, so too must firing always follow aiming, and precede it too, in order to make the necessary corrections ... Planners may be rightfully concerned about Rambo-type behaviour in management – "fire-fire-fire" in every direction, with no aiming. But managers must be equally wary of planning behaviour that amounts to "Ready. Aim. Aim."'

From *The Rise and Fall of Strategic Planning*

The author

Henry Mintzberg is professor of management studies at McGill University in Montreal, where he has been based since graduating with a doctorate from MIT in 1968. He also holds the title of visiting scholar at INSEAD in Fontainebleau, France.

Sources and further reading

Henry Mintzberg, 1994, *The Rise and Fall of Strategic Planning*, Free Press, New York.

Henry Mintzberg with JB Quinn, 1988, *The Strategy Process*, Prentice-Hall, Harlow (various editions since 1988).

Henry Mintzberg, July-August 1987, 'Crafting Strategy', *Harvard Business Review.*

This remains one of the most influential articles in its field and a true *Harvard Business Review* classic.

MARY MODAHL

Now or Never

2000

I t is a conceit of each passing business generation to imagine that it has to contend with the toughest trading and working conditions ever known. Compared to now, we say, didn't our parents have it easy back in the seventies, the eighties, the nineties …

Doubtless, children of the current business generation will have legitimate reasons for feeling they merit the accolade, but even they might concede that, looking back, the first decade of the twenty-first century was a particularly turbulent period.

From her perch as Vice-President of Research at Forrester Research Inc, a company at the forefront in providing research, analysis and advice on the business realities of new media and new technology, Mary Modahl is well placed to know what might lie ahead. Her view, explored in detail in *Now or Never*, is that the coming ten years will be a make-or-break period for many companies, well-established household names and business start-ups alike.

The growth in internet commerce, she says, is spawning a set of trends that all companies will have to confront. Some examples are:

- New pricing models undermine existing revenues, with many internet companies gambling that they can charge can lower prices and make up revenues on volume.
- Higher customer-service expectations. Internet businesses are open 24 hours a day, seven days a week, and so consumers can make purchasing choices at a time that suits them, having helped themselves to information about products before buying.
- New ways to distribute products. Internet companies build their businesses around home delivery – even in markets where home

delivery has never existed before. This has caught traditional companies, which focus on consumers' in-store experience, off guard.

- Unexpected market opportunities. Because the internet connects people across very wide distances at extremely low cost, start-ups can dream up services that literally were never possible before.
- High rates of entry – even in very staid markets. Conservative industries such as newspaper classified advertising, which had not seen a significant entrant in decades, find themselves challenged by newcomers.

These trends set the stage for the battle for internet consumers – a conflict, writes Modahl, 'that will span more than ten years as companies adjust their strategies to take advantage of the internet's ability to let consumers buy anytime, anywhere. On one side of this battle stand the established corporations – companies and brands that people have known since childhood. On the other stand the "dotcoms", start-ups that believe they can offer consumers a better deal and become a household name in the process.'

The battlefield is uneven, Modahl thinks: 'Start-ups, with their internet birthright, have the advantage. Being small, newer companies can move quickly, and their entire business revolves around a single focus. In addition, start-ups have had easy access to venture funding and more risk-tolerant investors than traditional companies. But most important, the dotcoms have nothing to lose if the old ways of doing business fade away.' In contrast, she says, 'traditional companies have developed a core of well-understood business practices. Although this core is valuable, it also creates a gravity field, trapping the company by continually pulling it back toward the way it has always done business.'

All, however, is not lost for the traditional companies. The internet changes many business rules, but some fundamentals remain – such as knowing the customer, adding real value, and differentiating from competitors. The successful companies, dotcom or traditional, Modahl believes, will be those – old or new – that can understand internet consumers, exploit internet business models, and defy the gravity of the old ways of doing business.

The crucial first step to success in the internet economy, she says, is understanding that the internet consumer is an entirely new entity. Modahl claims that conventional demographic methods, which segment populations according to their age, social grouping, or education, are poor predictors of online behaviour. Instead, drawing on research conducted by Forrester, she puts forward a system called 'technographics', which measures consumers' attitudes towards technology. One

Zeitbite

Success in the internet economy – the challenges

'Internet start-ups must grow at a breathtaking pace to support their investors' expectations. For these newly formed companies, there is no choice but to acquire customers and revenue as fast as possible – and most do so at the cost of ever-widening losses. Traditional players must defend their customer base as they try to re-gear their company around the new business models. In most cases, this makeover requires cutting prices, improving service, and reducing costs faster than ever before. In short, the internet makes consumer industries far more competitive and dynamic than they were in the past.

'As this day-to-day rivalry intensifies, it will become more important to step back and identify the sources of long-term value. Simply running like mad to sign up customers may be rewarded in the short run, particularly since the economies of scale in internet businesses are so pronounced. Gaining market share, however, is not enough. Internet businesses are not natural monopolies, and there is no rule that states that once a company has acquired its customers, it can relax and go back to pricing above cost. Entry barriers remain low, and the key assets that internet companies build – brand awareness and technological know-how – can be fumbled away in a single year.'

Taken from *Now or Never*

measure, for example, explores whether consumers feel positive or negative – Forrester found that 52% of the population is optimistic about technology and is 'marching happily towards online shopping'. Another crucial distinction is whether internet consumers are motivated by career, family or entertainment needs. Not surprisingly, income level is also a significant factor.

Putting these elements together, Modahl and Forrester have come up with ten types of internet consumer, including categories like the *Fast Forwards* (high-income optimists motivated by career needs), *Traditionalists* (high-income pessimists focused on nurturing their family and community relationships), *Media Junkies* (high-income pessimists focused on feeding their appetite for fun but who don't see technology as a way to met their needs), and *Sidelined Citizens*. The book contains extensive analysis to help the reader understand the drivers of the various groupings and how to target them.

The Forrester system of 'technographics' is the truly innovative part of *Now or Never*, but Modahl is equally sound writing on internet business models and offers convincing, research-based advice that enables readers to select which approach might suit their particular individual businesses.

All in all, *Now or Never* provides some thoroughly convincing models, ideas and practical advice on how to excel in the internet economy, and fully justifies Modahl as one of the most incisive analysts in the e-commerce field. And let's face it: those people working for companies that do succeed will have something to tell their children about.

The author

Mary Modahl is Vice-President of Research at Forrester Research Inc., a provider of primary research, market analysis, and strategic guidance in the area of electronic commerce. She is an influential and often-quoted industry figure whose work on the internet economy embraces media, interactive software technologies and business trade. She lives in Concord, Massachusetts.

Sources and further reading

Mary Modahl, 2000, *Now or Never: How companies must change today to win the battle for the Internet customer*, HarperCollins, New York.

GEOFFREY MOORE

Crossing the Chasm

1991

C anadian songwriter Leonard Cohen tells a story of a time some years back when he was on a ferry travelling between Greek islands. While wandering around on deck, he heard somebody with a guitar giving a rendition of *Suzanne*, one of his most popular songs, to a group of friends. Cohen says that was the moment when he knew that he no longer owned the song – it belonged to the world.

Geoffrey Moore might well feel the same about his most famous model – the Technology Adoption Life Cycle. First unveiled in *Crossing the Chasm*, the model describes five groups – Innovators, Early Adopters, Early Majority, Late Majority and Laggards – which are, in Moore's words, 'distinguished from each other by their characteristic response to a discontinuous innovation based on a new technology'. The model has been widely adopted and adapted, appearing in various guises. In her book *Now or Never*, for example, Mary Modahl of Forrester Research (see above) divides a company's consumer base into three categories – Early Adopters, Mainstream, and Laggards.

Like any model that has been widely used and popularized, sometimes the precision and intention of the original version gets overlooked. So it is worth reiterating Moore's model as it was intended. The first point to emphasize is that the model was conceived specifically for the hi-tech market. This is a critical component of understanding each profile and its relationship to its neighbours.

As to the five categories, Moore described them like this:

- *Innovators* pursue new technology products aggressively. They sometimes seek them out even before a formal marketing programme has been launched. This is because technology is a central interest in their life. At root they are intrigued with any fundamental advance and often make a technology purchase simply for the pleasure of exploring the new device's properties. There are not very many innovators in any given market segment, but winning them over at the outset of a marketing campaign is key nonetheless, because their endorsement reassures the other players in the marketplace that the product does in fact work.

- *Early Adopters,* like innovators, buy into new product concepts very early in their life cycle, but unlike innovators, they are not technologists. Rather they are people who find it easy to imagine, understand, and appreciate the benefits of a new technology, and to relate these potential benefits to their other concerns. Whenever they find a strong match, early adopters are willing to base their buying decisions upon it. Because early adopters do not rely on well-established references in making these buying decisions, they are key to opening up any high-tech market segment.

- The *Early Majority* share some of the early adopters' ability to relate to technology, but ultimately they are driven by a strong sense of practicality. They know that many of these new inventions end up as passing fads, so they are content to wait and see how other people are making out before they buy in themselves. They want to see well-established references before investing substantially. Because there are so many people in this segment – roughly one-third of the whole adoption life cycle – winning their business is key to any substantial profits and growth.

- The *Late Majority* share all the concerns of the early majority, plus one major additional one: whereas people in the early majority feel able to handle a technology product, should they finally decide to purchase it, members of the late majority are not. As a result, they wait until something has become an established standard, and even then want to see lots of support before they buy, typically from large, well-established companies. Like the early majority, this group comprises about one-third of the total buying population in any given segment. Courting this group is highly profitable, for while profit margins decrease as the products mature, so do the selling costs, and virtually all the R&D costs have been amortized.

- Finally there are the *Laggards.* These people simply don't want anything to do with new technology, for any of a variety of reasons, some personal and some economic. The only time they ever buy a technological product is when it is buried so deep inside another product – the way, say, that a microprocessor is designed into the braking system of a new car – that they don't even know it is there.

Laggards are generally regarded as not worth pursuing on any other basis.

Moore then sums up the five categories as follows:

Innovators	the technology enthusiasts;
Early Adopters	the visionaries;
Early Majority	the pragmatists;
Late Majority	the conservatives; and
Laggards	the sceptics.

These profiles provide the foundation of Moore's second key model, the High-Tech Marketing Model. That model says that the way to develop a high-tech market is to focus initially on the innovators, grow that market, then move on to the early adopters, grow that market, move on to the early majority, and so on through to the late majority, and even possibly to the laggards. Companies, says Moore, need to use each 'captured' group as a base for marketing to the next group, i.e. the innovators endorse a product and this becomes an important base from which a company can develop a credible pitch to the early adopters, the endorsement of the early adopters enables a pitch to the early majority, and so on.

It is, says Moore, 'important to maintain momentum in order to create a bandwagon effect that makes it natural for the next group to want to buy in. Too much of a delay, and the effect would be something like hanging from a motionless vine – nowhere to go but down.'

There is another good reason for keeping up the momentum: in Moore's words, this is 'to take advantage of your day in the sun before the next day renders you obsolete'. Portable electric typewriters, for example, were displaced by portable PCs, which in turn may lose out to internet terminals.

From this notion of having your day in the sun comes the idea of a *window of opportunity* – another of Moore's concepts for which he is rarely credited. If momentum is lost when a window of opportunity presents itself, then the chances are that a company will be overtaken by a competitor, 'thereby losing the advantages exclusive to a technology leadership position – specifically, the profit-margin advantage during the middle to late stages, which is the primary source from which high-tech fortunes are made'. This is the point at which a product 'crosses the chasm' of the book's title.

To summarize, the essence of the High-Tech Marketing Model is a smooth transition through all the stages of the Technology Adoption

Life Cycle. For those companies that get it right, writes Moore, the potential rewards are huge: 'What is dazzling about this concept, particularly to those who own equity in a high-tech venture, is its promise of virtual monopoly over a major new market development. If you can get there first, "catch the curve", and ride it up through the early majority segment, thereby establishing the defector standard, you can get rich very quickly and "own" a highly profitable market for a very long time to come.'

The author

Geoffrey A Moore is president of The Chasm Group, based in Palo Alto, California. The Chasm Group provides consultancy services to high-tech companies like Hewlett-Packard, Apple, PeopleSoft, AT&T, Oracle, Silicon Graphics and Sybase.

Sources and further reading

Geoffrey Moore, 1999, *Crossing the Chasm: Marketing and selling technology products to mainstream customers* (2nd edn), HarperCollins, New York. (The first edition was written in 1990 and published in 1991.)

Geoffrey Moore, 2000, *Living on the Faultline*, HarperCollins, New York.
Moore looks at the issue of managing for shareholder value in the age of the internet. Moore's prediction, and he's been right often enough to merit being taken seriously, is that the next big market is 'massive outsourcing that is web-enabled'.

Geoffrey Moore, 1998, *Inside the Tornado*, HarperCollins, New York.

Geoffrey Moore, Paul Johnson and Tom Kippola, 1998, *The Gorilla Game*, Capstone, Oxford.

The authors examine what makes a technology company a good investment bet. Being a clear architectural leader in its category is the key, coupled with good underpinning technology and operating practices within the company.

KENICHI OHMAE

The Mind of the Strategist

1982

S omebody once reported that the average human being has about 60,000 thoughts in a day. Unfortunately, it seems, over 99% of these thoughts are the same as the day before!

A key theme of Kenichi Ohmae's *The Mind of the Strategist* is that successful business strategies stem primarily from a creative mind rather than from a rote formula. Published in 1982 at a time when the rational school of strategy was still in the ascendant, Ohmae's thesis – that many people fail in strategy because they think of it as a tool rather than a state of mind – challenged widely held beliefs.

Successful business strategies, Ohmae writes, come from a thought process that is basically creative and intuitive rather than simply from step-by-step analysis: 'My message in this book ... is that successful business strategies result not from rigorous analysis but from a particular state of mind. In what I call the mind of the strategist, insight and a consequent drive for achievement, often amounting to a sense of mission, fuel a thought process which is basically creative and intuitive rather than rational ... Great strategies, like great works of art and great scientific discoveries, call for technical mastery in working out but originate in insights that are beyond the reach of conscious analysis.'

Although the central thrust of his book is that strategy Japanese-style is often irrational and non-linear, Ohmae does not entirely spurn some of the West's more conventional imagery of strategy as warfare. He is quite happy to describe strategy in the classic military sense as deploying forces to achieve a competitive advantage. 'In business as on the battlefield,' Ohmae writes, 'the object of strategy is to bring about the conditions most favourable to one's own side, judging precisely the right moment to attack or withdraw and always assessing the limits of compromise correctly. Besides the habit of analysis, what marks the mind of

Strategy defined by Kenichi Ohmae

'Strategy is defined as the way in which a corporation endeavours to differentiate itself positively from its competitors, using its relative corporate strengths to better satisfy customer needs ... Strategy is really no more than a plan of action for maximizing one's strengths against the forces at work in the business environment.'

Taken from *The Mind of the Strategist*

the strategist is an intellectual elasticity or flexibility that enables him to come up with realistic responses to changing situations, not simply to discriminate with great precision among different shades of grey.'

Ohmae's book was arguably the first solid call for integrative thinking in business, all the more remarkable considering that it was originally published in Japan in 1975. The strategist's job, he says, 'is very simply to challenge the prevailing assumptions with a single question: Why? and to put the same questions relentlessly to those responsible for the current way of doing things until they are sick of it'.

But *The Mind of the Strategist* delivers more than an exhortation to organizations to develop an idiosyncratic mode of thinking. Ohmae encourages organizations to devote attention to what he terms the 'Strategic Triangle'. As he puts it, 'in the construction of any business strategy, three main players must be taken into account: the corporation itself, the customer, and the competition'. Only by integrating the three Cs in a strategic triangle can sustained competitive advantage exist. In this context, the job of the strategist is 'to achieve superior performance, relative to competition, in the key factors for success of the business'. At the same time, he writes, 'the strategist must be sure that his strategy matches the strengths of the corporation with a clearly defined market. Positive matching of the needs and objectives of the two parties involved is required for a lasting good relationship; without it, the corporation's long-term viability may be at stake.'

Even though some of the examples Ohmae gives in his book now seem a bit dated, his thinking and ideas have held up remarkably well. *The Mind of the Strategist* oozes good sense and clear advice.

These days, Ohmae has bigger concerns on his mind than business. In his more recent books, he worries about globalization, about the impact of technology, about a new sort of cold war fought by businesses rather than governments, and about how best to educate citizens for this new world.

Zeitbites

'Merely allocating resources in the same way as your competitors will yield no competitive edge.'

'To formulate a corporate strategy that will be difficult for a competitor to imitate, the company either develops a completely new product or makes use of a position of relative superiority.'

'The true strategic thinker can respond flexibly to the inevitable changes in the situation that confronts the company. And it is that flexibility which, in turn, increases the chances of success.'

'In a free, competitive economic world, there will be no stability in a corporation's performance if it allows its attention to be diverted from the basic business mission of serving its customers.'

Taken from *The Mind of the Strategist*

The author

Kenichi Ohmae was born in 1943. He is, according to the *Financial Times*, 'a personality in a land where outspoken personalities are rare ... Japan's only management guru'. In 1994, *The Economist* selected him as one of five management gurus in the world.

For a period of 23 years, Ohmae, who has a doctorate from MIT, was a partner in McKinsey and Co., where he was a co-founder of its strategic management practice. He left McKinsey & Co. in 1995 to stand for the governorship of Tokyo. He has also played a vital role in assisting Asian governments to develop future-oriented regional strategies.

As an author he has produced over 100 books, many of which are devoted to business and socio-political analyses. He now lives in Tokyo.

Sources and further reading

Kenichi Ohmae, 1982, *The Mind of the Strategist*, McGraw Hill, New York.
Kenichi Ohmae, 2000, *The Invisible Continent*, HarperBusiness, New York.

According to Ohmae, the invisible continent is the world in which businesses now operate, which is like a new, just-discovered continent. The invisible continent has dimensions: the Visible Dimension – physical things to buy and make; the Borderless World – inevitable globalization; the Cyber Dimension – the internet, and mobile phones; and the Dimension of High Multiples.

Kenichi Ohmae, 1994, *The Borderless World: Power and Strategy in the Interlinked Economy*, HarperCollins, New York.

Ohmae argues persuasively how national borders are less relevant than ever before and identifies key characteristics of top-performing nations and corporations.

RICHARD PASCALE
& ANTHONY ATHOS

The Art of Japanese Management

1981

A s we know, the Second World War left Japan's economy and industrial base in tatters. The country's subsequent transformation into a major world competitor has been well documented. In particular, much has been made of the contribution made by American quality gurus like Deming and Juran, whose work was largely overlooked in their own country. In the later years of the twentieth century, the Japanese experienced huge success in markets which had previously been dominated by America or Europe, and they became dominating players in production fields such as copiers, motorcycles, small cars, heavy equipment, and consumer electronics.

During the 1980s and 1990s, Japan's management methods became the focus of a great deal of study. More than anybody, Richard Pascale and Anthony Athos were the people who brought the Japanese style of management to the attention of the western world, and made it a hot topic with their book *The Art of Japanese Management.*

At the time of writing their book, Pascale and Athos were both consultants for McKinsey and Co. They found that the more they worked with American companies and examined US working methods and practices, the more concerned they grew. Western management was hierarchical, and in large part modelled on military practices in terms of levels of authority, unity of command, line and staff functions, and so on. Decision-making was essentially top-down. Equally concerning to them was a level of self-confidence that existed in American companies that did not seem justified by corporate performance.

As they came increasingly to the view that sources of best management practice lay beyond rather than within US borders, they turned their heads to the more consensual working practices of Japan. Their research revealed some harsh truths about US industrial performance as they concluded that 'if anything, the extent of Japanese superiority over the United States in industrial competitiveness is underestimated'.

They found that managerial skill levels were higher in Japan than in the West, but perhaps most damning of all was their observation of western management that it had too many management tools at its disposal but displayed too little vision. They were concerned that western managers were beguiled by management fads and used them in a piecemeal and inauthentic manner. Japanese companies, in contrast, were visionary, and only deployed management tools that would advance them towards their chosen goals. Although the concept of vision is widely known nowadays, and having a vision is regarded by most organizations as essential, Pascale and Athos were the first writers to discover and champion the value of vision as a unifying, dynamic *modus operandi*.

However, for all that *The Art of Japanese Management* was the first widely read paean to the power of galvanizing, authentically held vision, the book is best known these days for hosting the first public appearance of the Seven S framework.

This framework, which now features as an element of just about every MBA programme running on the planet, was originally developed as a consulting tool for McKinsey & Co. in 1979 by a team that included Pascale, Athos, Robert Waterman and Tom Peters.

In essence, the Seven S model is a diagnostic tool that categorizes organizations into seven key areas of concern:

- *Strategy*: developing a strategy that moves towards a shared vision for the organization and matches its core competencies to the needs of the environment;
- *Structure*: ensuring that structure (how the firm is organized) supports the strategy;
- *Systems*: ensuring that systems (how information flows around the organization) also support the strategy;
- *Skills*: organizational capabilities and competencies;
- *Style:* management style and level of commitment to change (including the levels of openness and participation within the organization);
- *Shared values*: the culture, purpose and guiding precepts of the organization and how these are communicated both within the organization and to outsiders; and
- *Staff*: people issues such as the use of team work, empowerment and participation, reward and promotion issues.

Some of these areas are 'hard' (strategy, structure and systems) and some are 'soft' (style, staff and shared values). Skills is placed centre-piece because it is both 'hard' and 'soft', comprising both the distinctive capabilities of key personnel and the core competencies of the organization as a whole. The importance of the model lies not only in understanding each dimension within the framework but also in looking at the fit between the seven dimensions.

According to Pascale and Athos, the value of the Seven S model is that it imposes an interviewing discipline on researchers, forcing them to audit an organization from all perspectives, both 'hard' and 'soft'. The importance of the model lies not only in understanding each dimension within the framework but also in looking at the fit between the seven dimensions.

The Seven S model is a useful starting point in understanding organizational change because the model recognizes the complex inter-relationships that exist between different aspects of organizational life: on the one hand, the technical and operational aspects of providing a product or service; on the other hand, the rich human dimension that surrounds them. This is critical because it is in the ability to integrate the 'hard' and 'soft' aspects of organizational change that the best organizations often differentiate themselves.

Pascale and Athos conclude that Japanese companies were superior in skills, staff, shared values, and management style – all of which one might term the soft skills. In contrast, the West was preoccupied with the hard Ss of strategy, structure and systems.

Since the book was published, over 20 years ago, western companies have started to direct more attention to the soft Ss, with mixed success. What is ironic, of course, is that Japan's image as a role model for good managerial practice has been tarnished in recent years as its industrial performance has slipped.

The authors

Richard Pascale is an associate fellow of Oxford University. For 20 years, he was a member of the faculty at Stanford's Graduate School of Business. He has worked closely with the CEO and top management teams of many large corporations including AT&T, General Electric, *The New York Times*, British Petroleum, Ciba Geigy and Intel.

During his career, Anthony Athos worked for McKinsey & Co. and was professor of business administration at Harvard Business School.

Sources and further reading

Richard Pascale and Anthony Athos, 1981, *The Art of Japanese Management*, Penguin, London.

Richard Pascale, 1990, *Managing on the Edge: How successful companies use conflict to stay ahead*, Simon and Schuster, New York, (see below).

Richard Pascale, Mark Milleman and Linda Iona, 2000, *Surfing the Edge of Chaos*, Texere Publishing, London.

Tracy Goss, Richard Pascale and Anthony Athos, November/December 1993, 'The Reinvention Roller Coaster', *Harvard Business Review*.

Historically, companies in trouble have attempted various means of changing their fortunes. Many have been successful, but by the same token many have failed. This article explores why at least one of these tactics, reengineering, hasn't been as successful as it should have been in some situations.

RICHARD PASCALE

Managing on the Edge

1990

W e're all used to great opening lines in works of fiction. A good first sentence intrigues us and compels us to read on. It creates a mood, sets the tone of the book. Take the opening line from George Orwell's *1984*, for example: 'It was a bright cold day in April, and the clocks were striking thirteen.'

Now here's a challenge: how many management books have you read from which you can recall the opening line? Not many, I'll bet. To prove the point, here are a few examples from some of the best-selling management texts of all time:

- 'We had decided, after dinner, to spend a second night in Washington.' – *In Search of Excellence* by Peters and Waterman.
- 'In the world of institutions, commercial corporations are newcomers.' – *The Living Company* by Arie de Geus.
- 'Look around your company.' – *Competing for the Future*, Hamel and Prahalad.

In *Managing on the Edge*, Richard Pascale gives us, for my money, the best first sentence ever to feature in a management text (if you disagree, let me know your nomination).

It's succinct, and it acts as a verbal hologram for the entire book. And it goes like this: 'Nothing fails like success.'

Pascale is the most gnostic of management gurus. You can picture him as a Shaolin master, lecturing the young monks on the paradoxes of the world. In a *Star Wars* movie, he would be Yoda.

It's no coincidence that at about the same time as his former McKinsey & Co. colleagues Peters and Waterman were publishing *In Search of Excellence*, with its subtitle 'Lessons from America's best-run companies', Pascale and his co-author Anthony Athos were coming up with *The Art of Japanese Management*, a book that encouraged the West to look eastwards for the best examples of managerial practice (see above).

As you will have gathered by now, even if you haven't yet read one of his books, Pascale is not your typical American management guru. He teases the reader, rather than offering simplistic prescriptions. When he opines that nothing fails like success, in other words that great strengths are inevitably the root of weakness, he is having a dig at the Tom Peters school of thinking that sustainable business success can be built on the back of formulas and acronyms.

What Pascale does better than any other writer on the management block is to encourage readers to question their assumptions about the way organizations work. He writes about the need both to build and to break paradigms. Successful companies, he argues, need a good core paradigm, but the more successful it is, the less easy it is to let the paradigm go when the changing environment requires the organization to change.

Pascale characterizes nothing failing like success as a five-stage process. It begins with the organization coming up with a strategic concept, a product or service. Secondly, the organization organizes itself around that basic product or service, and in the process creates a culture and personality for itself. Thirdly, the company basks in the success that it enjoys on the back of providing good products or services and a good organizational 'fit'. However, after a while, the level of success enjoyed by the company begins to falter. Typically, the organization responds by tightening its grip on its basic success formula but at the same time makes a number of tweaks here and there. Typically, things don't get any better and the organization is tipped into the fifth stage, which Pascale calls 'excess'.

This is when an organization reaches a fork in the road. One road leads an organization to try to rediscover the original formula that brought it success in the first place. This often manifests itself as a 'back to basics' strategy. This approach works for a few organizations, says Pascale, but most need to embark on a process of transformation based on a radically different mindset.

He describes how Jack Welch of General Electric used to bring in the likes of McKinsey & Co. to help the company make major decisions because their outside view helped to free up internal thinking. Then Welch had a better idea: push executives to break through the paradigm themselves. He sent two teams to China. There, as strangers in a strange land, and unfettered by familiarity, their ideas roamed free. Back in the

US, each team was given four hours with the board to put forward its ideas. Result: a startling new level of thinking, teamwork, and executive ownership of ideas.

In a similar vein, Pascale encourages organizations to think differently about the future. Most companies, he argues, have a view of the future that is locked in the past. When Harry M Warner of the Warner Brothers movie studio was asked in 1927 about the possibility of films having a soundtrack, he declared, 'Who the hell wants to hear actors talk?' More recently Ken Olsen, president, chairman and founder of Digital Equipment Corp., said in 1977, 'There is no reason for any individuals to have a computer in their home.'

Warner and Olsen were guilty, says Pascale, of managing the future from the past.

Their view of what was possible in the future was hampered by their sense of what the past had taught them. Managers all too often fall into the same trap when in fact they should be following John Kennedy's example when he declared that America would put men on the moon and bring them home again safely by the end of the 1960s. Most of the technology required to achieve this goal simply didn't exist when Kennedy laid down the challenge. But the vision was compelling enough to generate the persistence and creativity needed to complete the task.

Pascale calls this process 'managing the present from the future'. It is as though there is a gap between the vision and present reality, which acts as a vacuum that 'sucks' the organization into the future. What prevents most organizations from achieving transformation is a lack of imagination. Pascale puts it like this: 'The trouble with "transformation" is that it has been relegated to the questionable status of muddled, New Age thinking. In part, this is because we keep trying to apply the tools of transformation without a corresponding shift in our managerial mindset. From the vantage point of the old mindset, the "technology" of transformation is not that new. But when approached with a new way of thinking, systematic application of the right tools and techniques yields transformation. It's really not as mysterious as it sounds.'

To achieve this sense of what futures are possible, Pascale says that organizations need to become 'engines of inquiry'. Above all, they need to encourage healthy debate, even contention, to generate the best solutions.

The book's sub-title is 'How the smartest companies use conflict to stay ahead' and Pascale uses Darwinian theory to back up his view. He cites the Law of Requisite Variety, which states that the survival of any organism depends on its capacity to cultivate (not just tolerate) variety in its internal structure. Failure to do so results in an inability

> **Zeitbite**
>
> 'The sobering truth is that our theories, models, and conventional wisdom combined appear no better at predicting an organization's ability to sustain itself than if we were to rely on random chance.'
>
> Taken from *Managing on the Edge*

to cope successfully with variety when it is introduced from an external source. For example, fish in a bowl can swim, breed, obtain food with minimal effort, and remain safe from predators. But such fish are extremely sensitive to the slightest changes. In contrast, fish in the sea have to work much harder to sustain themselves and they are subjected to many threats. But because they cope with more variation, they are more robust when faced with change.

Managers need to encourage autonomy and diversity within the organization to fuel the creative process. Naturally, this aspect is uncomfortable for many organizations because of the conflict that it necessarily implies. Yet, this constructive conflict is an essential part of the process of renewal. Rather than seeking to 'resolve' conflict, we need to embrace it. According to Richard Pascale, it is the process of harnessing this conflict that alerts us to 'the higher order of complexity that successfully managing the renewal process entails. This leads again to our managerial mindset, or "paradigm". It lays the foundation for exploring the limitations of the old, and for charting the frontiers of the new.' Elsewhere he writes that 'we must recognize that what until now have been regarded as hardships or chronic sources of aggravation are in fact the wellspring of organizational vitality'.

The process of harnessing constructive tension can only be done by the organization at the deepest and most fundamental of levels; by passionate commitment to core values and by establishing an environment of safety, integrity and trust for the people who work for it. It is at this level that the organization seeks to resolve the creative tension between its current reality and its vision.

It is fitting that *Managing on the Edge* should conclude with a section entitled 'The question is the answer', for in Pascale's world, life is all about challenging and extending one's choice of paradigms. More than any other strategist, he eschews simplistic solutions, offering in their stead something far more valuable – the means by which managers might take a few steps nearer to what he calls 'a way of thinking that is continually open to the next paradigm and the next and the next... '.

The author

Richard Pascale is an associate fellow of Oxford University. For 20 years, he was a member of the faculty at Stanford's Graduate School of Business. He has worked closely with the CEO and top management teams of many large corporations including AT&T, General Electric, *The New York Times*, British Petroleum, Ciba Geigy and Intel.

Sources and further reading

Richard Pascale, 1990, *Managing on the Edge: How successful companies use conflict to stay ahead*, Simon and Schuster, New York.

TOM PETERS & ROBERT WATERMAN

In Search of Excellence

1982

W ith the publication of *In Search of Excellence* in 1982, Tom Peters and co-author Bob Waterman changed the way organizations thought about themselves. Notions of embracing a paradoxical world of constant change, of providing exemplary customer service and of the need for high-speed response are now mainstream corporate thinking, but during the mid-1980s, when Peters was at the peak of his fame, the challenge he and Waterman laid down was enormous.

It was while they both worked at McKinsey & Co. in the 1970s that Peters met Waterman.

Their book emerged from a piece of collaborative research in which they put together a sample of 62 firms which they defined as excellent.

The sample included companies that were generally considered to be innovative and excellent. The emphasis was exclusively on big companies and included the likes of IBM, Hewlett-Packard, Wal-Mart and General Electric. Their sample also reflected the industries in which the authors had a particular interest.

On top of this, they imposed six financial performance measures:

- compound asset growth, 1961–1980;
- compound equity growth, 1961–1980;
- the average ratio of market value to book value, 1961–1980;
- average return on capital, 1961–1980 (net income divided by total invested capital, where invested capital consists of long-term debt, non-redeemable preferred stock, common stock and minority interests);
- average return on equity, 1961–1980; and
- average return on sales, 1961–1980.

In order to qualify as a top performer in an industry, a company had to have been in the top half of the industry in at least four of the six measures for the full 20-year period. Of the original 62 firms identified, 43 met the performance criteria.

Based on their studies of the 43 companies, Peters and Waterman identified eight crucial attributes that they felt characterized these 'excellent' companies. As they put it, 'the eight basics of management excellence don't just work because they work; they work because they make exceptional sense'. That said, they also acknowledged that employees in these companies had often been practising these basics without even knowing it.

Here are the eight attributes:

1   *A bias for action*: excellent companies 'do it, fix it, try it', say Peters and Waterman.
2   *Close to the customer*: 'excellent companies really are close to their customers. That's it. Other companies talk about it; the excellent companies do it.'
3   *Autonomy and entrepreneurship*: excellent companies have 'an ability to be big and yet to act small at the same time'.
4   *Productivity through people*: 'treat people as adults. Treat them as partners; treat them with dignity; treat them with respect. Treat them – not capital spending and automation – as the primary source of productivity gains.'
5   *Hands-on and value-driven management*: 'the real role of the chief executive is to manage the values of the organization'.
6   *Stick to the knitting*: excellent companies operate businesses that they know inside-out.
7   *Simple form, lean staff*: excellent companies 'have realized the importance of keeping things simple despite overwhelming pressure to complicate things'.
8   *Simultaneous loose-tight properties*: excellent companies are simultaneously centralized and decentralized, combining 'firm central direction and maximum individual autonomy'.

It's interesting to note how well these attributes have stood the test of time – rather better, it must be said, than many of the companies featured in the book! Very few modern-day CEOs would gainsay the list that Peters and Waterman came up with over 20 years ago.

Even so, *In Search of Excellence* did have some gaps in its thinking, as Peters acknowledged in an interview published in *Information Strategy* magazine in 1998: 'We got some stuff right, but we missed so much. You won't find information technology or globalization in the index. Yet, the odd thing is that the eight principles that we teased from the data were roughly right.' Peters expanded on this theme in a discussion with Kevin Kelly in the December 1997 issue of *Wired* magazine:

> *Kevin Kelly*: 'You published your first best-seller, *In Search of Excellence*, almost exactly 15 years ago. What would be different if you were writing it today?'
>
> *Tom Peters*: 'I would have focused a lot more on the information technology. It still amazes me after 15 years that I'm seen as a radical because, when I look back, I would guess that 90% of my errors have been errors of conservatism, not radicalism. But I guess it was a pretty radical message for the time, in a world that wasn't ready for globalization or the value of information. What I did focus on a lot in that book was the importance of pleasing customers. Even that was considered radical back then.'

Despite these comments by Peters, despite, indeed, his recent admission that some of the research data for the book was faked, and even though a number of the 'excellent' companies featured went on to suffer spectacular falls from grace, *In Search of Excellence* unquestionably deserves its place in our Ultimate Library. As the most popular management book of all time (world-wide sales to date have exceeded six million), it has influenced the thinking of a generation of managers. But perhaps the book's biggest and most long-lasting achievement is that it propelled customer service from a topic to which many companies did no more than pay lip service to a 'must-do' item at the top of the corporate agenda.

The authors

Tom Peters is probably the best-known management guru in the world. Other gurus like Peter Drucker have a faithful following but nobody can touch Peters for penetration of the management consciousness, and it was his collaboration on *In Search of Excellence* that propelled Peters onto the international stage in 1982. Peters was and remains an outstanding speaker and communicator. His disingenuous description of himself as a regular guy who 'just talks about stuff I've seen' underplays his unique ability to survey the business world, synthesize what he sees, and then present his findings in an accessible, vibrant and provocative way. Peters is the founder of the Tom Peters Company, with offices in Palo Alto, Boston, Chicago and London.

Bob Waterman has a less stellar profile than Peters. He has written two books, the most recent being *The Frontiers of Excellence*, published in 1994. He has a consultancy company based in California, although he apparently prefers to spend his time painting rather than performing on the seminar circuit.

Sources and further reading

Tom Peters and Robert Waterman, 1982, *In Search of Excellence*, Har-perCollins, New York.

Tom Peters, 1999, *The Brand You 50*, Knopf, New York.

This book sets out Peters's passionate belief that the individual has become the fundamental unit in the new economy. The book consists of, in his own words, '50 ways to transform yourself from an employee into a brand that shouts distinction, commitment and passion'. Stripped to their essence – decide what you want to do, and then do it obsessively – many of the ideas in the book are valid but, two years on from his *Fast Company* article, no longer particularly original.

Stuart Crainer, 1997, *Corporate Man to Corporate Skunk – a Biography of Tom Peters*, Capstone, Oxford.

For those interested in Tom Peters, Stuart Crainer's biography captures the man, his method and his impact on management thinking admirably. The book focuses on Peters's public life, hardly touching on his private affairs (a multi-millionaire who has been married four times). In doing so, it gives a clear and balanced appraisal of a man who is unquestionably a business phenomenon.

Tom Peters, August-September 1997, 'The Brand Called You', *Fast Company*.

The full title of this article is 'The brand called you: you can't move up if you don't stand out'. It's a brilliant synthesis of economic, marketing and business themes that ends with a stark conclusion: 'It's this simple: you are a brand. You are in charge of your brand. There is no single path to success. And there is no one right way to create the brand called You. Except this: Start today. Or else.'

Wired magazine, December 1997, in which Peters shares his thinking on a range of topics in a four-page interview with Kevin Kelly.

TOM PETZINGER

The New Pioneers

1999

T homas Petzinger spent 20 years as a journalist at *The Wall Street Journal*, before leaving in 2000 to set up his own business. His last four years at the paper were spent covering a rich variety of business stories, and conducting hundreds of face-to-face interviews with successful small business owners, which he featured in his weekly column called 'The Front Lines'.

In *The New Pioneers*, Petzinger describes how many of these interviews produced 'disorienting reporting experiences', which turned traditional business thinking on its head. People didn't just not do what the business books said they ought to do; more often than not, they were doing the complete opposite. And yet they were achieving astonishing success. This led Petzinger to conclude in his final Front Line column that 'in the new economy, everyone is an entrepreneur'.

This is how Petzinger characterizes new pioneers: 'Today's pioneers have embarked on a new frontier, some in search of riches, others in search of freedom, all in search of the new. Unlike the West of old this frontier is not one of place. It is a frontier of technologies, ideas, and values. The new pioneers celebrate individuality over conformity among their employees and customers alike. They deploy technology to distribute rather than consolidate authority and creativity. They compete through resilience instead of resistance, through adaptation instead of control. In a time of dizzying complexity and change, they realize that tightly-drawn strategies become brittle while shared purpose endures. Capitalism, in short, is merging with humanism.'

The New Pioneers, then, is about a revolution that Petzinger believes is quietly reshaping the face of American business and creating an opportunity-rich economy. This revolution is not to be found in the headline-grabbing mega-mergers, takeovers, downsizing, fiscal crises,

---

Zeitbite

'In 1962, while walking around the production factory at Non-Linear Systems with his tape recorder in his hand, Abraham Maslow dictated the following entry: "The most valuable one hundred people to bring into a deteriorating society ... would not be one hundred chemists, or politicians, or professors, or engineers, but rather one hundred entrepreneurs." In Maslow's time, entrepreneurs were much fewer in number, and almost none worked in major corporations. Today entrepreneurs abound, not just in small business but across the landscape of the corporate world. They have brought us this far, and they will take us further still.'

Taken from *The New Pioneers*

---

or bust-ups that dominate the front pages of the financial press; rather these changes are visible in the spectacular success enjoyed by a growing number of small and medium-sized firms.

At the heart of these firms' success, he argues, is an entrepreneurial outlook that is team-centred rather than self-centred. An open, selfless organization is not only good for the business, but also good for all involved, both inside and outside. Such an organization needs people who are individually passionate about what they do and who use all of their resources for the good of the team and of the wider company.

Petzinger puts forward a compelling case for small and medium-sized businesses being the engine-room of a new economy more often characterized as being populated by mega-corporations at one end of the scale or tiny start-ups or the other – what Charles Handy has called the world of elephants and fleas. Petzinger's focus on this middle group amounts to a revisionist statement.

At a deeper level, he is arguing for a fundamental shift in our collective thinking about the nature of organizations. Few people wake up on a Monday morning positively enthused about the prospect of going into work. And yet Petzinger has uncovered hundreds of small companies where people have a genuine desire to belong and to contribute, where individual capability is harnessed to a collective potential to create astonishing results.

Can small and medium-sized businesses retain this quality as they enjoy success and grow larger? Is big automatically bad? It would have been fascinating to see Petzinger really getting to grips with these questions.

Perhaps it is being churlish to criticize minor omissions when Petzinger gives us so much. *The New Pioneers* proves its own hypothesis that business with a human face can work as well as if not better than more traditional approaches brilliantly, employing a compelling mix of anecdotes and analysis. There is, though, just a nagging feeling that a little less story-telling and a bit more analysis and reflection might have made this an absolute classic.

The author

Thomas Petzinger worked at *The Wall Street Journal* for over 20 years, holding a variety of positions before leaving in 2000. For four years, he wrote a weekly column called 'The Front Lines'. He is a graduate of the Medill School of Journalism at Northwestern University. He recently created LaunchCyte Inc., a small business incubator based in Pittsburgh, Pennsylvania, of which he is Chairman and CEO.

He is author of *Hard Landing: The epic contest for power and profits that plunged the airlines into chaos* (Times Books, 1997).

Sources and further reading

Thomas Petzinger, 1999, *The New Pioneers: Men and women who are transforming the workplace and marketplace*, Simon and Schuster, New York.

Petzinger can be contacted by e-mail at tom@petzinger.com

The 'Petzinger Report' newsletter can be found at www.petzinger.com

B JOSEPH PINE II & JAMES H GILMORE

The Experience Economy

1999

 hy does a cup of coffee cost more from a trendy café than it does from a street vendor, or when it is made at home? Partly it's because of the inherent costs involved, but more significant is the nature of the experience and the value attached to it. So say Pine and Gilmore, who begin this fascinating book by taking the reader through the following life story of a coffee bean:

'Companies that harvest coffee or trade it on the futures market receive – at the time of this writing – a little more than $1 per pound, which translates into one or two cents a cup. When a manufacturer grinds, packages, and sells those same beans in a grocery store, turning them into a good, the price to a consumer jumps to between 5 and 25 cents a cup (depending on brand and package size). Brew the ground beans in a run-of-the-mill diner, corner coffee shop, or bodega and that service now sells for 50 cents to a dollar per cup. So depending on what a business does with it, coffee can be any of three economic offerings – commodity, good, or service – with three distinct ranges of value customers attach to the offering. But wait: serve that same coffee in a five-star restaurant or espresso bar, where the ordering, creation, and consumption of the cup embodies a heightened ambience or sense of theatre, and consumers gladly pay anywhere from $2 to $5 for each cup. Businesses that ascend to this fourth level of value establish a distinctive experience that envelops the purchase of coffee, increasing its value (and therefore its price) by two orders of magnitude over the original commodity.'

The coffee bean's journey from commodity, to good, to service, and finally to experience carries a telling moral: the most obvious and significant source of added value in this whole journey is the point at which the offering becomes an experience for the consumer.

It is this 'fourth level of value' that is the focus of *The Experience Economy*. It is at the experience level that companies have their biggest opportunity to distinguish themselves from their rivals.

The authors hold up Disney as a model provider of experiences. Disney's success, they suggest, can be attributed to the company's ability to sell indelible impressions, engage the senses to facilitate escapism, and create memories.

At the heart of success, say Pine and Gilmore, is a process that delivers a consistent, positive and memorable experience for the customer. They identify five design principles involved in creating a memorable experience:

1 *Theme the experience*: create a consistent and well-defined theme, one that resonates throughout the entire experience. Eat at the Hard Rock Café or TGI Fridays and you instantly know what to expect when you walk through the door.
2 *Harmonize impressions with positive cues*: while the theme is the foundation of the experience, impressions are the 'takeaways' that fulfil the theme. To create the desired impressions, companies must introduce cues that affirm the nature of the experience to the customer. As the authors put it, 'Even the smallest cue can aid the creation of a unique experience. When the restaurant host says "Your table is ready", no particular cue is given. But when a Rainforest Café host declares, "Your adventure is about to begin", it sets the scene for something special.'
3 *Eliminate negative cues*: crabby staff, long queues, unpleasant environments, intrusive announcements and other off-putting experiences. Unfortunately, the easiest way to turn a service into an experience is to provide poor service – thus creating, to quote the authors, 'a memorable encounter of the unpleasant kind'.
4 *Mix in memorabilia*: postcards, T-shirts and other souvenirs provide a physical reminder of the experience, and might influence customers to repeat the experience or, failing that, to share stories about their good experience with friends and colleagues.
5 *Engage the five senses*: the more all the senses are engaged, the more memorable the experience.

The authors warn that these five principles do not repeal the laws of supply and demand. An over-priced experience will struggle to attract repeat custom, no matter how well it is delivered. Likewise, over-capacity will see pressure on demand, pricing or both. Nonetheless, they believe that a growth in the experience economy is inevitable, mainly because it represents the best opportunity for a company really to distinguish itself in the eyes of its customers.

Though repetitious and at times verging on the metaphysical, *The Experience Economy* is crammed with illustrations and intriguing insights. From a new economy perspective, it would have been interesting to hear something from the authors about how the experience economy might operate in the on-line world; they do seem to have spent a lot of time in theme parks and restaurants, where the theatricality of experience shows through very easily. That said, Pine and Gilmore offer us another lens through which to view the future of commerce, and that in itself has value.

The authors

B Joseph Pine II and James H Gilmore are co-founders of Strategic Horizons LLP, a consultancy that aims to explore the frontiers of business and to help senior executives see the world differently.

Sources and further reading

B Joseph Pine II and James H Gilmore, 1999, *The Experience Economy: Goods and services are no longer enough*, Harvard Business School Press, Boston.

B Joseph Pine II and James H Gilmore, July-August 1998, 'Welcome to the Experience Economy', *Harvard Business Review.*
This article gives a good overview of the topic and may well cover it in enough depth for most people.

MICHAEL PORTER

Competitive Strategy

1980

Michael Porter is one of the pre-eminent names in strategic thinking, and quite possibly the most influential. His book *Competitive Strategy*, radical in its day, was one of the first to look at the whole field of competitive strategy. In it, he asked some key questions: What forces drive competition in an industry? How can a company be best placed to compete in the long run?

In the 20 years or so since *Competitive Strategy* was published, his body of work has entered and defined the strategic management mainstream. His techniques for analysing industries and competitors are now widely used. In fact, there probably isn't an MBA student in the world who won't be familiar with Porter's Five Forces Model and with his generic competitive strategies.

One of his most important contributions to the field of strategy is the concept of industry or 'structural' analysis, which seeks to explain the profit potential of different industries. The Porter Model states that the profitability of an industry is determined by five basic competitive forces:

1 the bargaining power of buyers relative to firms in the industry;
2 the bargaining power of suppliers relative to firms in the industry;
3 the ease of entry of new firms into the industry;
4 the availability of substitute products; and
5 the intensity of rivalry between existing firms in the industry.

The strength of the Five Forces Model is that it is rooted in economics and it enables an organization to analyse its performance in terms of:

- *the average profitability of the industry*, based on underlying economic and structural factors over which management has little control, at least in the short term; and
- *the management of the organization*: the difference between organizational performance and industry profitability that results from the way the organization is managed, the value of relationships built within and outside the industry, and other factors over which management *does* have control.

The model allows management to see what is possible in its industry and reduces the emotional factors that hinder an objective look at organizational performance. It is often an essential first step in strategic planning as it allows managers to begin to look at the big picture and put operational and day-to-day problems into perspective.

For many people, one big idea in a book would be plenty. However, in *Competitive Strategy*, Michael Porter sets out a second big idea. He argues that there are three fundamental ways (*generic* strategies) in which organizations can achieve sustainable competitive advantage:

1 *Cost leadership*: an organization sets out to become the lowest-cost producer in its industry. It does this by exploiting *economies of scale* or *scope* (including marketing and promotional expenditure necessary to maintain reputation or brand image) and the *experience/learning curve* (over time, experience results in better ways of doing things and hence lower costs). Cost leadership does *not* imply shoddy goods or poor quality, it simply means delivering goods and services to customers at the quality level expected at the lowest price (as determined by the customer!). It is perhaps better understood through the term *operational excellence*. An example of an organization pursuing this strategy is ASDA through its 'every-day low prices' strategy.

2 *Differentiation*: Porter defines differentiation as the ability to 'be unique in [the] industry along some dimensions valued by the customer'. This might be through technical innovation (*product or service leadership*) or through *customer intimacy* (understanding and knowing customers better than competitors).

3 *Focus*: choosing a narrow competitive scope within an industry by selecting a market segment or group of segments and serving customers in these segments to the exclusion of others.

Strategy defined by Michael Porter

'Developing a competitive strategy is developing a broad formula for how a business is going to compete, what its goals should be, and what policies will be needed to carry out those goals.'

Taken from *Competitive Strategy*

Since a focus strategy can be either cost-driven or differentiation-driven, Porter argues that there are essentially only *two* different generic strategic options: cost leadership, and differentiation.

Although later writers have sought to adapt these generic strategies to mirror the complexities that exist in the real world in order to provide some kind of new template for organizations making strategic choices, in truth, these templates add very little to Michael Porter's two fundamental strategies.

One of the reasons that Porter's generic strategies have held up so well over the years is that they are grounded in economics (the laws of supply and demand). Consumers will buy a given quantity at a given price, the price differential being equal to the perceived incremental added value of a particular organization's product or service. Where

---

Michael Porter's six principles of Strategic Positioning

1 The company must start with the *right goal*: superior long-term return on investment. Only by grounding strategy in sustained profitability will real economic value be generated. Economic value is created when customers are willing to pay a price for a product or service that exceeds the cost of producing it. When goals are defined in terms of volume or market share leadership, with profits assumed to follow, poor strategies often result. The same is true when strategies are set to respond to the perceived desires of investors.

2 A company's strategy must enable it to deliver a *value proposition*, or a set of benefits, different from those that competitors offer. Strategy, then, is neither a quest for the universally best way of competing nor an effort to be all things to every customer. It defines a way of competing which delivers unique value in a particular set of uses or for a particular set of customers.

---

3 Strategy needs to be reflected in a *distinctive value chain*. To establish a sustainable competitive advantage, a company must perform different activities to those performed by rivals, or perform similar activities in different ways. A company must configure the way it conducts manufacturing, logistics, service delivery, marketing, human resource management and so on differently from rivals and tailored to its own unique value proposition. If a company focuses on adopting best practices, it will end up performing most activities similarly to competitors, making it hard to gain an advantage.

4 Robust strategies involve *trade-offs*. A company must abandon or forgo some product features, services, or activities in order to be unique at others. Such trade-offs, in the product and in the value chain, are what make a company truly distinctive. When improvements in the product or in the value chain do not require trade-offs, they often become new best practices that are imitated because competitors can do so with no sacrifice to their existing ways of competing. Trying to be all things to all customers almost guarantees that a company will lack any advantage.

5 A strategy defines how all elements of what a company does *fit* together. A strategy involves making choices throughout the value chain that are interdependent; all a company's activities must be mutually reinforcing. A company's product design, for example, should reinforce its approach to the manufacturing process, and both should leverage the way it conducts after-sales service. Fit not only increases competitive advantage but also makes a strategy harder to imitate. Rivals can copy one activity or product feature fairly easily, but will have much more difficulty duplicating a whole system of competing. Without fit, discrete improvements in manufacturing, marketing or distribution are quickly matched.

6 Strategy involves *continuity* of direction. A company must define a distinctive value proposition that it will stand for, even if that means forgoing certain opportunities. Without continuity of direction, it is difficult for companies to develop unique skills and assets or build strong reputations with customers. Frequent corporate 'reinvention', then, is usually a sign of poor strategic thinking and a route to mediocrity. Continuous improvement is a necessity, but it must always be guided by strategic direction.

Derived from *Competitive Strategy*

there is no perceived added value in the eyes of the customer ('commodity products'), customers tend to buy on price alone. The tendency for companies to replicate the added-value features of competitive products tends to result in the 'commoditization' of products and services over time and an increasing sensitivity to price (for example, dairy products such as yoghurt, consumer products such as nappies, and financial services such as banking).

Although Porter's generic strategies can appear simplistic to the sophisticated managerial eye, the complexity lies in the translation of these strategies into competitive advantage. A differentiation strategy, for example, requires an organization to develop a distinctive strategic positioning based on strengths such as unique products, proprietary content, distinctive physical activities, superior product knowledge, and strong personal service and relationships. Porter defines six principles of Strategic Positioning that a company needs to follow.

A more valid debate is whether Michael Porter's concept of sustainable competitive advantage really exists. There is no doubt that consistently superior returns exist in the short to medium term but it is much rarer over the longer term. Some organizations do achieve consistently higher returns. However, this is based on the ability of these companies to re-invent themselves continually and to build new capabilities/core competencies rather than relying on existing strengths (demonstrated by the high percentage of sales derived from products less than two years old in these companies).

Many have argued that the introduction of the internet into business practices renders the old rules of strategy and competitive advantage obsolete. According to Porter, the opposite is true. In a *Harvard Business Review* article called 'Strategy and the Internet', he wrote that 'the only way [for companies to be more profitable than the average performer] is by achieving a sustainable competitive edge – by operating at a lower cost, by commanding a premium price, or by doing both'.

Because the internet tends to weaken industry profitability without providing proprietary operational advantages, it is more important than ever for companies to distinguish themselves through strategy. The winners will be those that view the internet as a complement to, not a cannibal of, traditional ways of competing.

Many of the early internet pioneers, both the newly minted dotcoms and those well-established companies seeking an on-line presence, have competed in ways that violate nearly every principle in the strategy rulebook. As Porter puts it: 'Rather than focus on profits, they have chased customers indiscriminately through discounting, channel incentives, and advertising. Rather than concentrate on delivering value that earns an attractive price from customers, they have pursued indirect revenues such as advertising and click-through fees. Rather than make trade-offs they have rushed to offer every conceivable product or service.'

The good news is that it did not have to be this way – these were bad strategic choices but they were not the only options available. And these choices had little to do with the inherent business potential of the internet. In fact, when it comes to reinforcing a distinctive strategy, Porter maintains that the internet provides a better technological platform than any previous generation of IT.

For most existing industries and established companies, the internet rarely cancels out important sources of competitive advantage; if anything, it is more likely to increase the value of those sources. But over time, says Porter, the internet itself will be neutralized as a source of advantage as all companies embrace its technology.

At which point, we may well see a return to the good old days when competitive advantages will once again explicitly derive from traditional strengths such as unique products, proprietary content, and distinctive physical activities. Internet technology may be able to fortify those advantages, but it is unlikely to supplant them.

The message, then, is clear. Gaining competitive advantage in the post-internet business world does not require a radically new approach to business; and it certainly does not require the abandonment of classic economic principles that can still offer strategic value in a marketplace that depends on cutting-edge information technology.

No, gaining competitive advantage in the early years of the twenty-first century is still reliant on applying proven principles of effective strategy as set out by Porter in *Competitive Strategy*. Sources of strategic advantage rest where they always have – in cost competitiveness, product differentiation, ease of entering exiting markets, and so on. It is perhaps Porter's crowning achievement that he has given the business world that rarest of gifts – models and concepts that have stood the test of time.

The author

Michael Porter is a professor at Harvard Business School, where he has worked since the 1970s. His first degree was in aerospace and mechanical engineering, and his doctorate was in industrial economics. *Competitive Strategy* was Porter's first book: it is now in its 53rd printing and has been translated into 17 languages.

Sources and further reading

Michael Porter, 1980, *Competitive Strategy*, Free Press, New York.

Michael Porter, 1998, *On Competition*, Harvard Business School Press, Boston.

Michael Porter, March 2001, 'Strategy and the Internet', *Harvard Business Review*.

Porter debunks such internet myths as first-mover advantage, the power of virtual companies, and the multiplying rewards of network effects. He disentangles the distorted signals from the marketplace, explains why the internet complements rather than cannibalizes existing ways of doing business, and outlines strategic imperatives for dot-coms and traditional companies.

Michael Porter, November/December 1996, 'What is Strategy', *Harvard Business Review*.

In this article Porter defines the difference between operational effectiveness and strategic positioning. An organization can outperform rivals only if it can establish a difference that it can preserve. It must deliver greater value to customers or create comparable value at a lower cost, or do both.

FREDERICK REICHHELD

The Loyalty Effect

1996

T hese days, the concept of loyalty seems quaintly old-fash-
ioned.

In the workplace, there are worrying signs that employee
loyalty has disappeared in a suicide pact with the job for life.
Countless employee surveys show that people are increasingly distrust-
ful of their companies, and feel disinclined to tie their personal future
to the future of their organization. Or as a bond dealer once memorably
put it to his employer: if you want loyalty, get a dog.

Meanwhile, investors have turned into hyperactive speculators,
more than willing to up sticks and take their money elsewhere at the
first hint of corporate difficulty. And as for customers, they have never
been so disloyal as in this era of vast consumer choice.

The sum total of this *tsunami* of fickleness is that, on average, US
corporations lose around half of their customers in five years, half of
their employees in four years, and half of their investors in under one
year.

Frederick Reichheld, director emeritus of Bain & Company, doesn't
accept any notion that loyalty is 'so twentieth century'. 'Loyalty is by no
means dead', he writes in *The Loyalty Effect*, 'In fact, the principles of
loyalty ... are alive and well at the heart of every company with an enduring record of high productivity, solid profits, and steady expansion'. He
claims that companies which ignore loyalty issues – whether they apply
to customers, employees or investors – are heading for a dismal future
of low growth, weak profits, and reduced life expectancy.

So what steps can a company that wants actively to address loyalty-
related issues take? Reichheld suggests that a loyalty-based strategy has
eight elements:

Can you tell your barnacles from your butterflies?

In the customer loyalty stakes, Frederick Reichheld draws a distinction between 'barnacles', who cling to the ship but slow its progress, and 'butterflies', who alight for seconds before flitting off.

The challenge in managing 'butterflies', i.e. customers who are profitable but disloyal, is to milk them for as much as you can while they're buying from you. For profitable customers who are likely to stay loyal, a softly-softly approach is more appropriate. These, says Reichheld, are 'true friends'.

When it comes to the 'barnacles', i.e. loyal but not very profitable customers, the challenge is to find out whether they have any potential to spend more than they currently do.

For 'strangers', who generate no loyalty and no profits, the approach is fairly obvious: identify them as early as possible and don't invest anything.

1 *Building a superior customer value proposition*: loyalty is generated by offering genuinely better value than competitors' offerings.
2 *Finding the right customers*: this often depends more on the magnetism of the value proposition and the positive word-of-mouth generated rather than flashy salesmanship.
3 *Earning customer loyalty*: treat customers like assets – use techniques such as pricing policies and service level commitments to help retain those assets.
4 *Finding the right employees*: be selective. Look for people with the required talent and skills who share the company's values and enshrine them in their behaviour.
5 *Earning employee loyalty*: invest heavily in training and development. Construct career paths, make jobs more satisfying. Reflect higher productivity in higher pay.
6 *Gaining cost advantage through superior productivity*: the productivity surplus generated by better customer and employee loyalty creates a cost advantage. Structure incentive so that employees treat spending company money as though they are spending their own cash.
7 *Finding the right investors*: as far as possible, pursue non-traditional capital structures such as mutual or private ownership. For public companies, the challenge is to attract that rare breed – investors with a long-term perspective.

8 *Earning investor loyalty*: investors must earn a decent return on their cash before management starts paying itself bonuses. Company employees should treat investor money with the same care that would be given to their own cash.

Battle-hardened corporate types might look at Reichheld's eight-point list and conclude that he is not exactly at the rocket-science end of management thinking.

Funnily enough, Reichheld would agree: 'These are certainly not fresh ideas … All are now clichés'. But, as with so many aspects of business life, the real trick of it lies in taking these concepts from rhetoric to reality. The journey is worth it, says Reichheld, because these ideas 'make money – more money in the long run than the cynical and opportunistic strategies we see all around us'.

The author

A graduate of Harvard College and the Harvard Business School, Frederick Reichheld is a director of Bain & Company, a leading strategy consulting firm based in Boston, where he leads the firm's worldwide Loyalty Practice.

Sources and further reading

Frederick Reichheld, 1996, *The Loyalty Effect*, Harvard Business School, Boston.

Frederick Reichheld, 1996, *Loyalty Rules!*, Harvard Business School, Boston.

Werner Reinartz and Viswanathan Kumar, July 2002, *Harvard Business Review.*

A fascinating extension of Reichheld's thinking. Simply put: not all loyal customers are profitable, and not all profitable customers are loyal. The traditional tools for segmenting customers are not very effective at identifying the latter group, causing companies to chase expensively after initially-profitable customers who do not hold much promise of future profits. The authors suggest an alternative approach, based on what they call 'event-history modelling' techniques, which more accurately predicts future buying probabilities.

JONAS RIDDERSTRÅLE & KJELL NORDSTRÖM

Funky Business

2000

O
n the face of it, a business book by two Swedish professors about how successful companies differ from their competitors doesn't sound like the most riveting of reads. But *Funky Business* is no dry theoretical tome; and authors Ridderstråle and Nordström are not your standard-issue academics. Unless, that is, it's normal for Swedish business professors to shave their heads, wear leather trousers, describe themselves as funksters, and call their public appearances gigs rather than seminars.

Perhaps it *now* sounds like you are in for a trip through some familiar corners of the modern business world in a lightweight and gimmicky manner redolent of Tom Peters at his worst, i.e. paddling at the shallow end. Far from it. This book draws extensively from rigorously researched data but presents its findings with wit and intelligence reinforced with excellent examples.

Ridderstråle and Nordström are convinced that we are moving towards a state of super-capitalism, with near friction-free markets. As a result, every supplier everywhere has access to the same resources, ideas, methods and technology. The catch is that every consumer now has access to fantastic choice.

In such a world, they say that time and talent are the two critical commodities and it is how companies deal with these two factors that determines which companies fall by the wayside and which move through to the next round. The goal, and this is as good as it gets, is to be, as the authors put it, 'momentarily ahead of the game'.

The authors offer a theoretical model for achieving this fleeting competitive advantage in the form of Funky Inc., a company that is flat, open, and small. It's a company in which, to take only a few samples from the *Funky Business* smörgåsbord, you would:

Zeitbite

The Funky Business *guide to leadership and management*

'This is the age of time and talent, where we are selling, exploiting, organizing, hiring and packaging time and talent. The most critical resource wears shoes and walks out the door around five o'clock every day. As a result, management and leadership are keys to competitive advantage. They differentiate you from the mass. How you attract, retain and motivate your people is more important than technology; how you treat your customers and suppliers, more important than technology. How a company is managed and how a company is led are vital differentiators. They can create sustainable uniqueness. But at the same time as management and leadership have reached maturity as potent competitive weapons, their very nature has changed.

'The boss is dead. No longer can we believe in a leader who claims to know more about everything and who is always right. Management by numbers is history. Management by fear won't work. If management is people, management must become humanagement.

'The job is dead. No longer can we believe in having a piece of paper saying job description at the top. The new realities call for far greater flexibility. Throughout most of the twentieth century, managers averaged one job and one career. Now, we are talking about two careers and seven jobs. The days of the long-serving corporate man, safe and sound in the dusty recesses of the corporation, are long gone. Soon the emphasis will be on getting a life instead of a career, and work will be viewed as a series of gigs or projects.

'Inevitably, new roles demand new skills. Thirty years ago, we had to learn one new skill per year. Now, it is one new skill per day. Tomorrow, it may be one new skill per hour. Skills like networking – in 1960, the average manager had to learn 25 names throughout their entire career; today we must learn 25 new names every single month. Tomorrow, it may be 25 new names per week.'

Taken from *Funky Business*

• Signal what you stand for in terms of values (i.e. branding) and then take those values with you on a trip of relentless innovation and change.

- Recognize that being average is not good enough: the goal is to be 100% completely right for a specific market, not ordinary and 95% right for everybody.
- Change the frame of reference from what you are selling to what the customer is actually buying – the two are not always the same! Get on the same 'vibe' as your customer.
- Take risks, accept and even welcome failure, and spurn all things average.
- Offer products and services that constantly take the customer by surprise. For example, on-line bookseller bol.com's 'Free copy for a friend' week, which ran in June 2000, increased sales three-fold with a campaign that emphasized giving a present rather than receiving a freebie. Claimed as a global first, when customers bought a CD or book from the top 40, they could nominate a friend who was sent a copy at no charge.
- Bring your products to market faster than anybody else, and replace them frequently. Most of Hewlett-Packard's revenues, for example, derive from products that are less than a year old.
- Use your core competencies to enter new industries without hesitation.

It is not easy to characterize *Funky Business*. The book overflows with provocative ideas, but it is not a practical 'how to survive the future' road map; nor is it a set of predictions on 'what the future will be like'. It is a comprehensive and coherent philosophy – the philosophy of FUNK. Unusually, in an age of instant gurus and ready prescriptions, Ridderstråle and Nordström leave it unambiguously up to the reader to embrace, integrate and apply the thinking contained in the book.

The authors

Jonas Ridderstråle is based at the Institute of International Business at the Stockholm School of Economics. He is on the boards of directors of Stokke Fabrikker, Swedish internet company Spary Ventures, and the US digital change agent Razorfish.

Kjell Nordström is based at the Centre for Advanced Studies in Leadership at the Stockholm School of Economics. In his spare time he is an art collector. He holds an MBA and a doctorate.

Sources and further reading

Jonas Ridderstråle and Kjell Nordström, 1999 (first published in the UK in 2000), *Funky Business*, ft.com, London.

You can visit the funksters at www.funkybusiness.com

PETER SCHWARTZ

The Art of the Long View

1991

ou don't need me to tell you that globalization and technology are sweeping away the market and industry structures that have historically defined competition. Swept away with them are the classic approaches to corporate strategy, nearly all of which mistakenly assume that a predictable path to the future can be paved from the experience of the past. In this turbulent world, companies must let go of the notion that strategic outcomes can be predetermined and that enduring competitive advantage can be defined and achieved.

Companies must instead adopt a 'portfolio-of-initiatives' approach, which bases new business opportunities on 'advantages of familiarity', on the continuous appraisal of initiatives, and on just-in-time decision making. This emphasis on strategic opportunism does not necessarily imply that detailed analysis is no longer necessary in the strategic process. There will always be a need for an objective evaluation process that ensures that the organization has been through a logical sequence of steps designed to think through the ramifications of a decision. But the primary purpose of this process should be to probe and challenge assumptions, surface mental models or mind-sets that are shared by those in the decision-making process, and to ask the 'what if' and 'why not' questions that extend the boundaries of organizational awareness.

This is also the basis for scenario planning, which constructs a series of possible future realities and examines the ramifications of each scenario on the organization. It is also the basis for the increasing use of 'micro-worlds', which use the power of information technology to do the same thing.

When it originally appeared, *The Art of the Long View* was one of the first books to explain and generally demystify the scenario planning techniques developed at Royal Dutch/Shell in the 1970s and 1980s.

Zeitbite

'Scenarios are a tool for helping us to take a long view in a world of great uncertainty. The name comes from the theatrical term "scenario" – the script for a film or play. Scenarios are stories about the way the world might turn out tomorrow, stories that can help us recognize and adapt to changing aspects of our present environment. They are a method for articulating the different pathways that might exist for you tomorrow, and finding your appropriate movements down each of those possible paths.'

From *The Art of the Long View*

Peter Schwartz led the scenario planning unit there for four years in the early eighties, and so he writes from a background of significant personal experience.

In *The Art of the Long View*, he describes how, in practice, scenarios resemble a set of stories, written or spoken, built around carefully constructed plots. 'Scenarios are stories that give meaning to events', says Schwartz. They are an old way of organizing knowledge; when used as strategic tools, they confront denial by encouraging – in fact, requiring – the willing suspension of disbelief. Stories can express multiple perspectives on complex events.

Creating scenarios, says Schwartz, requires decision-makers to question their broadest assumptions about the way the world works. Good scenarios are plausible, surprising, and have the power to break old stereotypes. Using scenarios is 'rehearsing the future' such that, by recognizing the warning signs, an organization can adapt, and act effectively. As Schwartz puts it, 'decisions which have been pre-tested against a range of what fate may offer are more likely to stand the test of time, produce robust and resilient strategies, and create distinct competitive advantage. Ultimately, the result of scenario planning is not a more accurate picture of tomorrow but better thinking and an ongoing strategic conversation about the future.'

The author

Peter Schwartz is co-founder and chairman of Global Business Network, an international think tank and consulting firm based in California. He is an internationally renowned futurist and business strategist.

His current research and scenario work encompasses energy resources and the environment, technology, financial services, telecommunications, media and entertainment, aerospace, national security, and the Asia-Pacific region. From 1982 to 1986, he led the scenario planning unit for the Royal Dutch/Shell group of companies in London.

Sources and further reading

Peter Schwartz, 1991, *The Art of the Long View*, Doubleday, New York.

Peter Schwartz, 1999, *When Good Companies Do Bad Things*, John Wiley, New York.

An exploration of business ethics at companies such as Nestlé, Texaco, Union Carbide, Nike and Royal Dutch/Shell.

PETER SENGE
The Fifth Discipline
1990

Peter Senge's book was one of the first to popularize the concept of the learning organization. According to Senge, learning organizations are 'organizations where people continually expand their capacity to create the results they truly desire, where new and expansive patterns of thinking are nurtured, where collective aspiration is set free, and where people are continually learning to see the whole together'. His rationale for such organizations is that, in times of constant change, only those that are flexible, adaptive and productive will thrive.

The Fifth Discipline emerged from extensive research by Senge and his team at MIT. As the title of his book suggests, Senge proposes that there are five components to a learning organization – personal mastery, mental models, shared vision, team learning, and systems thinking. Let's take each in turn:

- *Personal mastery.* Taking personal responsibility for ourselves is part of a wider discipline of personal growth and learning that is called personal mastery. Personal mastery does not imply dominance over other people. It is a journey on which we move from seeing ourselves as victims of external circumstances, over which we have little or no control, to an acceptance that we are each masters of our own destiny. It is also a discipline because it requires both a framework and a lot of hard work in the form of repeated practice. It may not be easy but the reward is high. It allows us to create our future, and with it the future of our organizations. Peter Senge relates this to the building of a 'learning organization' as follows: 'Personal mastery goes beyond competence and skills, though it is grounded in competence and skills. It goes beyond spiritual unfolding or opening, although it requires spiritual growth. It means approaching one's life as a creative work, living life from a creative as opposed to a reactive viewpoint ... People with high levels of personal mastery are continually expanding their ability to create the results in life they truly seek. From their quest for continual learning comes the spirit of the learning organization.'

It can be both ironic and frustrating that such a critical part of the change process remains firmly outside the control of those in charge of organizations. Often managers ask how they can get their employees to 'buy in' to a change process. The simple answer is that they can't. We don't commit ourselves to a change imposed on us externally; we cope with that change. We choose to participate if the change excites us and leads us to where we want to be, and we feel safe in the process.

- *Mental models.* Mental models are 'deeply ingrained assumptions, generalizations, or even pictures and images that influence how we understand the world and how we take action'. Because mental models lie well below the surface of our general awareness, we don't always realize the impact they have on our behaviour. But think about it: if you hold the belief that all *Sun* readers are morons, how does that affect the way you react if somebody walks into the room holding that particular newspaper?

  The start-point with mental models is for us to turn the mirror on ourselves, and to bring our assumptions to the surface so that we can hold them rigorously to scrutiny. The challenge for an organization wanting to move in the right direction is to reveal its current mental models in order that it might transcend the sorts of internal politics and game playing that can hamper performance.

- *Shared vision.* Organizations which have fostered genuinely shared visions can, and do, create their futures, *sometimes against overwhelming odds,* by mobilizing the resources and commitment of their most valued assets, the people within them. Shared vision provides the emotional and intellectual energy for the strategic journey to bridge the gap between what is and what could be. Senge summarizes the position as follows: 'At the heart of building shared vision is the task of designing and evolving ongoing processes in which people at every level of the organization, in every role, can speak from the heart about what really matters to them and be heard.'

  This symbiotic relationship between vision and awareness is captured by Senge: 'Many who are otherwise qualified to lead fail to do so because they try to substitute analysis for vision. They believe that, if only people understood current reality, they would surely feel the motivation to change. They are disappointed to discover that people "resist" the personal and organizational changes that must be made to alter reality. What they never grasp is that the natural energy for changing reality comes from holding a picture of what might be that is more important to people than what is. But creative tension cannot be created from vision alone; it demands an accurate picture of current reality as well. Vision without an understanding of reality will more likely foster cynicism than creativity. The principle of creative tension teaches that an accurate picture of current reality is just as important as a compelling picture of a desired future.'

Senge talks of the process as 'lining up all the arrows', making sure that the energy of individuals is flowing in the same direction so that it complements itself and contributes to the overall vision of the organization. In this sense, alignment is all about freeing the flow, so that individual energies can be liberated in the service of a common objective. Senge writes: 'In a corporation, a shared vision changes people's relationship with the company. It is no longer "their company"; it becomes "our company". A shared vision is the first step in allowing people who mistrusted each other to begin to work together. It creates a common identity.'

- *Team learning.* When teams learn together, not only can there be good results for the organization, but also individuals grow more rapidly, as well as feeling that they belong to something meaningful. Senge puts it like this: 'When you ask people about what it is like being part of a great team, what is most striking is the meaningfulness of the experience. People talk about being part of something larger than themselves, of being connected, of being generative. It becomes quite clear that, for many, their experiences as part of truly great teams stand out as singular periods of life lived to the fullest. Some spend the rest of their lives looking for ways to recapture that spirit.'

  At the heart of team learning is the process of dialogue, the capacity of members of a team to suspend assumptions, to move – as Senge puts it – from a spirit of advocacy to a spirit of enquiry.

- *Systems thinking.* Systems thinking is the fifth discipline, the conceptual cornerstone of Senge's model. It is the discipline, he writes, that 'integrates the others, fusing them into a coherent body of theory and practice'.

  In organizations, all too often, simplistic frameworks are applied to what are complex systems. We focus on the parts rather than the whole, on the short-term rather than long-term impact, and generally fail to see organization as a dynamic process. We think that cause and effect will be near to one another but, says

> ## Strategy defined by Peter Senge
>
> 'Thinking strategically starts with reflection on the deepest nature of an undertaking and on the central challenges that it poses.'
>
> From *The Fifth Discipline*

Senge, 'we never directly experience the consequences of many of our most important decisions'.

For example, cutting back on R&D, or advertising budgets, or training and development investment can bring very quick cost savings, but can severely damage the long-term viability of an organization. Senge concludes: 'The systems viewpoint is generally oriented toward the long-term view. That's why delays and feedback loops are so important. In the short term, you can often ignore them; they're inconsequential. They only come back to haunt you in the long term.'

When assessing Senge's significance, it is tempting to dismiss the learning organization as a pie-in-the-sky concept. The reality is that there are very few organizations that come close to possessing the characteristics that Senge identifies with the learning organization. Companies' priorities are overwhelmingly financial and short-term. These conditions are not conducive to building the sort of organization that Peter Senge proposes. In short, the learning organization is a great concept, but simply too idealistic.

This assessment seems too harsh, for there are some currents running in Senge's favour. In particular, the growing focus on knowledge management in an increasingly globalized economy might well lead organizations back to focusing attention on the development and growth of the people who have to create intellectual capital in the first place.

The author

Peter Senge was born in 1947; he graduated in engineering from Stanford and then went on to take a Masters on social systems modelling at MIT before completing his PhD on Management. He is now the director of the Centre for Organizational Learning at the Sloan School of Management, Massachusetts Institute of Technology. In 1999, he was named a 'Strategist of the Century' by the *Journal of Business Strategy*, one of 24 men and women who have 'had the greatest impact on the way we conduct business today'.

Sources and further reading

Peter Senge, 1990, *The Fifth Discipline: The art and practice of the learning organization*, Doubleday, New York.

Peter Senge et al., 1994, *The Fifth Discipline Fieldbook: Strategies and tools for building a learning organization*, Doubleday, New York.

Peter Senge et al., 1999, *The Dance of Change: The challenges of sustaining momentum in learning organizations*, Doubleday/Currency, New York.

The website www.fieldbook.com is home to *The Fifth Discipline Fieldbook Project* – it includes material from some of Senge's books.

CARL SHAPIRO & HAL R VARIAN

Information Rules

1998

'Annual income twenty pounds, annual expenditure nineteen nineteen and six, result happiness. Annual income twenty pounds, annual expenditure twenty pounds ought and six, result misery.'

Charles Dickens, *David Copperfield*

r Micawber's model of economic prudence, that being in profit mattered, has long since been banished to the realms of Dickensian quaintness. 'How unsophisticated', said the credit card generation. 'How unnecessary', commented the internet start-ups.

New century: new economy; new economics. When, early in 2000, lastminute.com's flotation gave it the same market value as venerable bricks-and-mortar retailer WH Smith, it did seem to confirm that the economic paradigm had been shifted by the upstart online businesses. Don't worry about this year's numbers, just imagine the potential a few years down the road. Share prices soared.

Then the markets tumbled, and a series of high-profile dot-com humiliations confirmed that the internet's period of grace is over. So what is the lesson from all this?

The easy answer is that profits still matter. A broader message comes from the authors of *Information Rules*, Carl Shapiro and Hal R Varian: ignore basic economic principles at your own risk. Technology changes. Economic laws do not.

Their book, highly rated by Kevin Kelly among others, sets out to show that classic economic principles can still offer strategic value in a marketplace that depends on cutting-edge information technology.

Zeitbite

What makes Shapiro and Varian's approach different from others?

'First, this book is not about trends. Lots of books about the impact of technology are attempts to forecast the future. You've heard that work will become more decentralized, more organic, and more flexible. You've heard about flat organizations and unlimited bandwidth. But the methodology for forecasting these trends is unclear; typically, it is just extrapolation from recent developments. Our forecasting, such as it is, is based on durable economic principles that have been proven to work in practice.

'Second, this book is not about *vocabulary*. We're not going to invent any new buzzwords (although we do hope to resurrect a few old ones). Our goal is to introduce new terms only when they actually describe a useful concept; there will be no vocabulary for the sake of vocabulary. We won't talk about "cyberspace," the "cyber economy," or cyber-anything.

'Third, this book is not about *analogies*. We won't tell you that devising business strategy is like restoring an ecosystem, fighting a war, or making love. Business strategy is business strategy and though analogies can sometimes be helpful, they can also be misleading. Our view is that analogies can be an effective way to *communicate* strategies, but they are a very dangerous way to analyse strategies.

'We seek models, not trends; concepts, not vocabulary; and analysis, not analogies. We firmly believe the models, the concepts, and the analysis will provide you with a deeper understanding of the fundamental forces at work in today's high-tech industries and enable you to craft winning strategies for tomorrow's network economy.'

Taken from *Information Rules*

The result is a book that is rigorous with its analysis, convincing in its grip of the subject (the authors are both *bona fide* economists), and oozing *gravitas*.

That said, Shapiro and Varian do lighten the challenge for the reader by supplementing their analysis with plenty of real-life examples.

Among the issues they explore are: pricing and versioning information; rights management; recognizing and managing lock-in; switching costs; and how to factor government policy and regulation into strategy. They conclude each section with a set of lessons derived from their analysis. For example, they offer the following pieces of advice on the matter of pricing information:

- analyse and understand how much you invest in producing and selling your product;
- if you are forced to compete in a commodity market, be aggressive but not greedy;
- differentiate your product by personalizing the information and the price;
- invest in collecting and analysing data about your market;
- use the information about your customers to sell them personalized products at personalized prices; and
- analyse the profitability of selling to groups, e.g. site licences.

These pointers might seem a little glib on their own but, unlike some other texts, their advice is merely a top-cut of findings that are substantiated elsewhere in the book.

Information Rules is not by any means an easy read but it is accessible to the general reader who is prepared to concentrate a bit. Highly recommended for chastened dot-com businesses.

The authors

Carl Shapiro is the Transamerica Professor of Business Strategy, Haas School of Business and Department of Economics, University of California at Berkeley. During 1995/96, he served as deputy assistant attorney-general for economics, in the Antitrust Division of the US Department of Justice.

Hal R Varian is the Class of 1944 Professor and the Dean of the School of Information Management and Systems, with joint appointments at the Haas School of Business and the Department of Economics, University of California at Berkeley.

Sources and further reading

Carl Shapiro and Hal R Varian, 1999, *Information Rules: A strategic guide to the network economy*, Harvard Business School Press, Boston.

Co-author Hal Varian oversees a website called *The Information Economy*, which lists hundreds of papers, works in progress, and links to other new economy websites. An almost overwhelming resource but one that hasn't been bettered. www.sims.berkeley.edu/resources/infoecon/

DAVID SIEGEL

Futurize your Enterprise

1999

'E veryone understands that the internet is changing business', says Siegel in *Futurize your Enterprise*, 'but most companies still don't understand how to approach the web. They've applied new kinds of marketing and technology, they've put their catalogues online, they put '.com' at the end of their names, and they have little to show for their efforts. That's because the limiting factor online isn't technology, branding, or bandwidth – it's mindset.'

According to Siegel, many companies fail to understand fully how e-commerce works, and as a result they fall into some or all of what he calls 'the six common traps of e-commerce', which are:

1 *Not taking the medium seriously*: for example, some companies treat the web like a trade show or simply an extension of their paper catalogues, or they simply copy their competitors. It almost seems more important to look as if they know what they're doing than actually to know.

2 *Trying to please everyone*: for example, packing the website with so many features that the customer is baffled. In trying to please everybody, the website satisfies nobody.

3 *Focusing on technology, rather than people*: you can tell how far your company has fallen into the technology trap by how long it takes to make a change on the site. If it's easy to make changes to the home page, that's a good sign. If it takes seven days to correct a spelling error, the technology is more of a barrier than an aid.

4 *Focusing on brands and messages*: for example, when companies go down this route, all too often the site is over-controlled and carries too much bland content. Customer comments are discouraged in case they are critical – the site is run by spin doctors.

5 *The introverted website*: this results when the site is organized around internal issues rather than needs of customers.

6 *Taking themselves too seriously*: this is being so intent in putting in place the content that the company believes the customer ought to want to know about that (a) the site seems pompous and humourless and (b) the real interests of customers are never known because nobody actually bothers to ask the question that really matters.

Futurize your Enterprise is really about how a company can avoid these traps and, more positively, become a meaningful player in what Siegel calls the Customer-Led Revolution that will connect almost two billion people to the web by the year 2010. The book is organized in four parts.

- In Part I, Siegel shows how companies like Microsoft and Dell have reorganized around customer groups – rather than around product, content, or service offerings – and this structure allows those companies to listen and respond to customer needs faster. 'In the next five years', he writes, 'those who understand the internet will reorganize around their most profitable customer groups and change their companies from the outside in. Microsoft recently made this transition. I believe most companies will learn from their experience and follow suit.' Siegel concludes this part by defining the Truth Economy, in which honest, open companies prosper while companies with something to hide are ignored or attacked.

- In Part II of the book, he outlines the six meetings that he believes are necessary to build a proper support system for a customer-led website. The meetings revolve around gaining internal commitment, customer segmentation, actively listening to customers, developing appropriate measures, customer modelling, and mapping out a strategy for implementation.

- In the third part, probably the most useful part of the book, Siegel takes us through eight fictitious case studies, covering various prototype businesses like a book superstore, a grocery store, a drug manufacturer. The case studies demonstrate clearly how properly-aligned, customer-led companies use the internet to benefit employees and customers equally. The keys to success seem to revolve around ongoing dialogue with customers, having employees who are empowered to respond to new demands, and putting in place processes that enable on-line businesses to follow customer behaviour and needs closely.

Zeitbite

'The first printed books imitated handwritten manuscripts. The first photographs were portraits. Many early motion pictures captured theatrical plays on screen. So it's not surprising that in the late 1990s, companies tried hard to re-create their familiar business environments online. They thought the world-wide web would provide the new "front-end" to their existing business practices. Re-creating the physical world online is a temporary, transitional and often unnecessary strategy.'

Taken from *Futurize your Enterprise*

- In the final section, Siegel offers some predictions about how the business landscape might develop over the next ten years, as most of the world goes online. He does this by creating a number of internet-user categories such as The Job Seeker, The Student, The Homemaker, and The Lawyer, and then speculating about how the internet might evolve for people in these categories.

Futurize your Enterprise is packed with insights and provocative assertions about the future shape of the internet. The book is a real wake-up call for companies who think that the internet is just starting to settle into recognizable business patterns, and that their on-line presence can be run using the same management mindset that runs the bricks-and-mortar business.

The author

David Siegel is chairman of Studio Verso, a web-design and strategy company, and president of Siegel Vision, an e-strategy company. His clients include Hewlett-Packard, Lucent, Sony and NASA. He serves as advisor to the HTML and STYLE committees of the W3C, a consortium in charge of further development of standards on the web. His previous books include *Creating Killer Web Sites* and *Secrets of Successful Web Sites*.

Sources and further reading

David Siegel, 1999, *Futurize your Enterprise: Business Strategy in the Age of the e-customer*, John Wiley, New York.
Futurize your Enterprise comes in seven parts. Four of them are in the book, and the other three are online at www.Futurizenow.com. The website has an online bootcamp for executives, updated links, and ongoing discussions. Worth investigating.

Siegel features in the March/April 2000 issue of the *Harvard Business Review* as the lead responder for that issue's case study.

THOMAS STEWART
Intellectual Capital
1997

ime was when capital could be viewed in purely financial or physical terms – it showed up in the buildings and equipment owned, it could be found in the corporate balance sheets. In recent years, though, the search has been on for an altogether more elusive, intangible form of asset: intellectual capital.

Intellectual Capital by Thomas Stewart has proved itself in the marketplace as the definitive guide to understanding and managing intangible assets. In it, the author provides a framework for, practical guide to, and theory of the significance of intellectual capital, which is defined by Stewart as 'packaged useful knowledge'.

Intellectual capital can be broken down into three areas:

* *Human capital*, which is the knowledge that resides within the heads of employees that is relevant to the purpose of the organization. Human capital is formed and deployed, writes Stewart, 'when more of the time and talent of the people who work in a company is devoted to activities that result in innovation'. Human capital can grow in two ways: 'when the organization uses more of what people know, and when people know more stuff that is useful to the organization'. Unleashing the human capital resident in the organization requires 'minimizing mindless tasks, meaningless paperwork, unproductive infighting'.

    However, human capital, as well as being needed by the organization, also has a value for the individual worker. In 1994, Peter Drucker wrote that 'the true investment in the knowledge society is not in machines and tools but in the knowledge of the knowledge worker ... The industrial worker needed the capitalist infinitely more than the capitalist needed the industrial worker ... In the knowledge society the most probable assumption for organizations – and certainly the assumption on which they have to conduct their affairs – is that they need knowledge workers far more than knowledge workers need them.'

- *Customer capital*, which is the value of a company's ongoing relationships with the people or organizations to which it sells. Indicators of customer capital include market share, customer retention and defection rates, and profit per customer. Stewart's belief is that 'customer capital is probably – and startlingly when you think about it – the worst-managed of all intangible assets. Many businesses don't even know who their customers are.'
- *Structural capital*, which is the knowledge retained within the organization that becomes company property. Stewart calls this 'knowledge that doesn't go home at night'. Structural capital 'belongs to the organization as a whole. It can be reproduced and shared.' Examples of structural capital include technologies, inventions, publications, and business processes.

Understanding what intellectual capital amounts to is only part of the story for organizations. The real value comes from being able to capture and deploy it. To this end, Stewart offers the following ten principles for managing intellectual capital:

1 Companies don't own human and customer capital. Only by recognizing the shared nature of these assets can a company manage and profit from them.
2 To create human capital it can use, a company needs to foster teamwork, communities of practice, and other social forms of learning.
3 Organizational wealth is created around skills and talents that are proprietary and scarce. To manage and develop human capital, companies must recognize unsentimentally that people with these talents are assets to invest in. Others are costs to be minimized.
4 Structural assets (those intangible assets the company owns) are the easiest to manage but those that customers care least about.
5 Move from amassing knowledge just-in-case to having information that customers need ready-to-hand, and that which they *might* need within reasonable reach.
6 Information and knowledge can and should substitute for expensive physical and financial assets.
7 Knowledge work is custom work.
8 Every company should re-analyse the value chain of the industry that it participates in to see what information is most crucial.

Zeitbite

'Knowledge assets, like money or equipment, exist and are worth cultivating only in the context of strategy. You cannot define and manage intellectual assets unless you know what you want to do with them.'

Taken from *Intellectual Capital*

---

9   Focus on the flow of information not the flow of materials.
10 Human, structural and customer capital work together. It is not enough to invest in people, systems and customers separately. They can support each other or detract from each other.

Since *Intellectual Capital* first appeared, there has been a flood of books on knowledge management hitting the marketplace. In an age of lightweight books on the new information age, this book is a heavyweight which not only explains why intellectual capital will be the foundation of corporate success in the new century, but also offers practical guidance to companies about how to make best use of their intangible assets.

The author

Thomas A Stewart is a member of the board of editors of *Fortune* magazine. He pioneered the field of intellectual capital in a series of articles that earned him an international reputation, the Planning Forum calling him 'the leading proponent of knowledge management in the business press'. He lives in Manhattan.

Sources and further reading

Thomas A Stewart, 1997, *Intellectual Capital: The new wealth of organizations*, Doubleday, New York.
Thomas A Stewart, 2001, *The Wealth of Knowledge*, Nicholas Brealey, London.

DON TAPSCOTT
Digital Capital
2000

hen we compiled the list of books to feature in *The Ultimate Strategy Library*, one of our easiest decisions was to include 'the latest Tapscott'.

The phrase is significant. Many business writers seem content to produce one decent book with some worthwhile ideas, but they then rehash and repackage the material in subsequent books – the law of diminishing authorial returns. Tapscott is different: with each new book he goes deeper into the heart of the new economy.

Digital Capital, co-written with two colleagues, explores how the net and digital media open up new ways to create wealth. It features companies like Shwab, eBay, Cisco, MP3 and Linux, which have transformed the rules of competition in their industries by making revolutionary offerings to their customers. They did not achieve this alone: combining with like-minded partners with complementary skills was the key.

Tapscott, Ticcoll and Lowy call these internet-based partnerships or alliances 'business webs', or 'b-webs' for short. A b-web, according to the authors, is 'a distinct system of suppliers, distributors, commerce services providers, infrastructure providers and customers that use the internet for their primary business communications and transactions'. Although alliance-based, a b-web typically has an identifiable lead partner which formally orchestrates the b-web's strategies and processes.

The core of *Digital Capital* is devoted to describing five distinct types of b-web:

- *Agoras.* The agoras of ancient Greece were centres for public intercourse and commercial transactions. The authors apply the term to 'markets where buyers and sellers meet to freely negotiate and assign value to goods'. Price discovery mechanisms include one-to-one haggling, multiparty auctions and exchanges. An example of an Agora is eBay, the internet-based consumer auction website.

- *Aggregations.* 'In an aggregation b-web, one company – like Wal-mart – leads ..., positioning itself as a value-adding intermediary between producers and customers.' The lead aggregator selects products and services, targets particular market segments, sets prices and ensures fulfilment. Retailers and wholesalers are examples of aggregations.
- *Value chains.* The lead organization structures a b-web network to produce a highly integrated value proposition. The output satisfies a customer order or market opportunity and the seller has the final say in pricing.
- *Alliances.* 'The most ethereal of b-webs', alliances aim for high-value integration without a formal hierarchy of control. Alliances include online communities, research initiatives, and shared experiences. The MP3 phenomenon is an Alliance.
- *Distributive networks.* These are the b-webs that, in conjunction with the roads, postal and telephones services, and power grids of the industrial economy, keep the new economy alive and mobile. They don't create or consume their cargo – they simply pass it around. Examples include data network operators, the new logistic companies and on-line banks.

The authors go on to outline the following six-step process for 'weaving a b-Web':

1 *Describe the current value proposition from the customer's viewpoint,* that is, why this system exists.
2 *Disaggregate*: consider the contributors and their contributions, strengths and weaknesses. Compare the parts and capabilities of your business to those in other systems.
3 *Envision b-web-enabled value* through brainstorming and other creative design techniques. Decide what the new value proposition will be.
4 *Reaggregate*: define what it will take to deliver the new value proposition, including processes, contributors, contributions, applications and technologies, and other success factors.
5 *Prepare a value map*: design a visual map that depicts value exchanges in the b-web.
6 *Do the b-web mix*: define a b-web typing strategy that will improve your competitive advantages.

The new alphabet of marketing

The A, B, C, D, E of marketing has replaced the four Ps:

- *Anyplace, anytime, anyway shopping replaces place.* Companies must design integrated strategies for the marketspace and, if appropriate, the marketplace and marketface. Customers want convenience;
- *B-web customers drive revenue.* Relationship capital is reflected in a brand. Think of customers as part of your b-web and prospects as candidates for relationships, not as markets for your products;
- *Communication works, not promotion.* One-way media, like broadcasting, can be part of the marketing mix, but the customer decides whether – and with whom – to engage in a one-, two-, or multi-way communication;
- *Discovery of price replaces fixed price.* The days when companies unilaterally control prices are nearly over; and
- *Experience replaces product.* Customers pay for experiences, not products. Products must be bundled with enhanced, customized services. The automobile experience replaces the product, as the vehicle becomes a platform for transportation, interactive entertainment, safety, doing business, and having fun.

Taken from *Digital Capital*

Reading *Digital Wealth* reinforces a sense that Tapscott's understanding deepens with each new book that he (with or without collaborators) publishes. Where this book differs from the majority is that it goes beyond mere description, beyond eye-catching but slight lists of key points (don't be misled by the précis above – there is substantial analysis and commentary underpinning each point). When it comes to characterizing what is driving change in the economy, there are hundreds of books on the market. *Digital Capital* goes well beyond the simplistic sloganizing to offer genuine insight and, even more important, some guidance on practical steps that can be put in place.

The authors

Don Tapscott is chairman, David Ticoll is CEO, and Alex Lowy is managing director of the Alliance for Converging Technologies, an international research and consulting group that advises corporations and governments worldwide on strategy in the digital economy.

The authors can be contacted on digitalcapital@actnet.com

Sources and further reading

Don Tapscott, David Ticoll and Alex Lowy, 2000, *Digital Capital: Harnessing the power of business webs*, Nicholas Brealey, London.
The Alliance for Converging Technologies has a website, which can be found at www.actnet.com

Don Tapscott, 1996, *The Digital Economy: Promise and peril in the age of networked intelligence*, McGraw-Hill, New York.
Explores some of the emerging dynamics of the new economy. More examples than theory or analysis, but good at picking out business trends.

Don Tapscott, 1998, *Growing up Digital: The rise of the net generation*, McGraw-Hill, New York.
Explains how, as it grows up, the net generation is learning to communicate, work, shop, and play in new ways by using the internet as a basic resource. It is aimed at businessmen, parents and teachers, giving them some pointers about how to plan for the future.

N oel Tichy thinks that managers and consultants all too often limit their ability to manage change because of a tendency to focus attention on a familiar but restricted set of organizational change levers. Why does this matter? The point is that the way that we choose to view the underlying facets of change issues affects the actions that we take, and the solutions that we employ. In an organization, an inappropriate intervention that fails to recognize the full complexity of an issue is most likely to make a problem worse and not better.

Tichy argues that looking at a problem systemically will always yield a better understanding than simply leaping in with all preconceptions blazing. Considering that it was back in the 1930s that researchers began to look at businesses not just as technical or economic institutions, but also as social systems, it has taken a long time for organizations to recognize and come to terms with the fact that they have both rational and non-rational underpinnings.

According to Tichy, managing strategic change raises some fundamental questions about the nature of organizations. What business or businesses should we be in? Who should reap what benefits from the organization? What are the values and norms of organizational members?

Managing Strategic Change sets out Tichy's conceptual framework for managing these basic dilemmas and problems facing organizations in three key areas (or systems) – the technical, political, and cultural. He calls his framework TPC theory after these three areas, which he believes pose fundamental problems for organizations that 'require continuous attention', and which are 'never solved, but constantly adjusted over time'.

Tichy uses a powerful analogy of the intertwined strands of a rope to demonstrate how the technical, political and cultural systems play out in an organizational setting. He makes the point that, just as it is virtually impossible to distinguish the individual strands of a rope from a distance, so it is difficult to distinguish an organization's technical, political and cultural systems. He also points out that ropes can weaken and unravel over time; the same is true of organizations.

When the technical, political and cultural systems are not working together harmoniously, the organization becomes weakened. It is the process of strategic management that is supposed, in Tichy's words, to keep the 'rope together in the face of changing demands brought on by technical, political, and cultural changes in the environment'.

Perhaps it would be useful at this point to say a little more about each of the three systems:

- *Technical system*. This refers to how an organization faces production problems, and how technical resources along with people and money are arranged to produce the desired output. Methods and techniques used to tackle these problems are goal setting, strategy formulation, organization design and management systems.
- *Political system*. Tichy uses this term to describe how an organization addresses the problem of allocating power, influence and resources. Other relevant factors are the use to which the organization will be put, as well as determining who will (and who won't) reap the benefits. The political area has less formalized rules than the technical system and usually 'less overt concepts and language' are associated with the political system.
- *Cultural system*. Tichy notes that culture is the 'normative glue' that in part holds an organization together. The organization needs to establish what norms and values should be held by its members. Since organizations are continually in flux, these norms and values must repeatedly align internally and with their external environments.

The effectiveness of these three systems is determined by the extent to which there is alignment within and across each system. The key to managing strategic change effectively is to align an organization's components, that is, its mission and strategy, its structure, and its human resources, and to do this within the technical, political and cultural systems.

What becomes clear from reading *Managing Strategic Change* is Tichy's view that change is multifaceted and paradoxical and that change management is now a major portion of virtually every manager's role. Given that effective diagnosis is the basis for any managed change effort, TPC theory offers the reader a framework for addressing change issues in a systematic and thorough manner. With his concept of the strategic rope, Noel Tichy has come up with possibly the most potent strategic metaphor of the past 25 years.

The author

Noel Tichy is professor of organizational behaviour and human resource management at the University of Michigan Business School. He has been a member of the faculty at Michigan since 1980. Prior to that, he was an associate professor at Columbia University (from 1972 to 1980), and a senior research associate at the Centre of Policy Research (from 1970 to 1980). He received a PhD from Columbia University in 1972.

He serves on the board of governors of the American Society for Training and Development, and is editor-in-chief of *Human Resource Management Journal*.

Sources and further reading

Noel Tichy, 1983, *Managing Strategic Change: Technical, political and cultural dynamics*, John Wiley, New York.

Noel Tichy and Ram Charan, 1998, *Every Business is a Growth Business*, Times Books/Random House, New York.

Noel Tichy and Eli Cohen, 1997, *The Leadership Engine: How Winning Companies Create Leaders at All Levels*, HarperCollins, New York.

Noel Tichy and Stratford Sherman, 1993, *Control Your Destiny or Someone Else Will: How Jack Welch is Making General Electric the World's Most Competitive Company*, Doubleday/Currency, New York.

ALVIN TOFFLER
The Third Wave
1980

T he 'Third Wave' referred to in the title of Alvin Toffler's classic is the age of 'the super-industrial society' in which the new technologies redefine how people operate at a societal, organizational and personal level. Following two preceding waves (the agricultural phase of civilization's development, followed by the 'second wave' of industrialization), the Third Wave, Toffler anticipated, would bring with it much anxiety and trauma. It would be characterized by great uncertainty. 'Old ways of thinking', he writes, 'old formulas, dogmas, and ideologies, no matter how cherished or how useful in the past, no longer fit the facts'. He continues, 'the world that is fast emerging from the clash of new values and technologies, new geopolitical relationships, new lifestyles and modes of communication, demands wholly new ideas and analogies, classifications and concepts'.

Given that the reputation of all futurologists hangs on the accuracy of their predictions, it is instructive to examine how elements of Toffler's view of the future compares to what has actually unfolded over the past two decades:

- 'The essence of Second Wave manufacture was the long "run" of millions of identical standardized products. By contrast, the essence of Third Wave manufacture is the short run of partially or completely customized products,' wrote Toffler. Mass production has increasingly yielded pride of place to the concept of mass customization to the extent that the latter now dominates most traditional mass production industries such as car manufacture.
- 'The customer will become so integrated into the production process that we will find it more and more difficult to tell just who is actually the consumer and who is the producer,' said Toffler. Online

banking services, and Amazon's customers contributing book reviews are just two examples where customers now routinely do 'work' on behalf of companies they deal with.

- Toffler believed that, as well as its traditional commercial focus, the organization of the future would be greatly concerned with a range of social, ecological, moral and political problems. There has been no significant sign of this happening on a voluntary basis, despite or possibly due to the degree of change that has occurred within organizations.
- 'Machine synchronization shackled the human to the machine's capabilities and imprisoned all of social life in a common frame. It did so in capitalist and socialist countries alike. Now, as machine synchronization grows more precise, humans, instead of being imprisoned, are progressively freed,' said Toffler. He rightly predicted the demise of the traditional nine-to-five working day, and the move towards flexible working patterns, without necessarily picking up on the fact that growing numbers of organizations would move to 24/7 working patterns.
- Toffler predicted the 'de-massifying' of our culture. The growth of tribalism, the expansion of local TV and radio media, and greater personalization of communication services (for example, the availability of video-on-demand down telephone lines) all point to cultural fragmentation.
- The Third Wave, he wrote, 'will produce anxiety and conflict as well as reorganization, restructuring, and – for some – rebirth into new careers and opportunities. The new systems will challenge all the old executive turfs, the hierarchies, the sexual role divisions, the departmental barriers of the past.' These 'new systems' can be seen in a number of trends and phenomena that have impacted on working life over the past 20 years, for example empowerment, process reengineering, the flattening of hierarchies, downsizing, house-husbands, the demise of the job-for-life, and portfolio working.

Toffler spends a significant chunk of *The Third Wave* exploring how organizations and organizational life might change. 'Instead of clinging to a sharply specialized economic function, the corporation, prodded by criticism, legislation, and its own concerned executives, is becoming a multipurpose institution', he writes. He identifies five forces that will impact on organizations, namely changes in:

1 the physical environment;
2 the 'line-up of social forces';

3 the role of information;
4 government organization; and
5 morality.

Reading *The Third Wave* 20 years after its first publication is a curious experience. On one hand, the book remains very contemporary in feel, and his profile of the new economy is a pretty close match. On the other hand, when he gets down to the level of describing the nuts and bolts of technology to come, the book seems remarkably dated. For example, at one point he goes into some detail to describe what a word processor is. Perhaps though, that should merely serve to remind us how rapidly wave upon wave of technological innovation have come at us, and how, as Shoshana Zuboff once wrote, 'patterns of morality, sociality and feeling are evolving much more slowly than technology'.

The Third Wave has proved to be a largely accurate depiction of a future that has now more or less reached us. Given the status it has achieved, it seems all the more remarkable that it is currently virtually impossible to locate a copy in a bookstore – either bricks-and-mortar or on-line. Maybe the future isn't what it used to be.

The author

A former Washington correspondent and editor of *Fortune* magazine, Alvin Toffler is a highly respected futurologist. He has served briefly as a visiting professor at Cornell University and a visiting scholar at the Russell Sage Foundation. He holds five honorary degrees.

Sources and further reading

Alvin Toffler, 1980, *The Third Wave*, Bantam, New York.
Alvin Toffler, 1970, *Future Shock*, Bantam, New York.
   Close to three decades ago, Toffler anticipated the waves of anxiety that the technological revolution would engender in this ground-breaking exploration of what happens to people and society when overwhelmed by change.
Shoshana Zuboff, September 1995, 'The Emperor's New Workplace', *Scientific American*.
   An insightful piece about the impact of technology on the workplace.

SUN TZU
The Art of War
500 BC

lthough his identity is shrouded in mystery, Sun Tzu is believed to have been the commander-in-chief in China's kingdom of Wu some 2,500 years ago.

The Art of War is essentially a compilation of advice for dealing with battle situations.

Sun Tzu's book is credited with being the first formalized strategy text. Its significance today rests in the widely-held view that the concepts and principles of war and military strategy are still highly relevant, not only in military circles but also in business management.

For example, Sun Tzu advises that leaders must continually change how they attack the competition, because if their actions are predictable, their opponents can easily defeat them. He writes: 'Therefore, when I have won a victory I do not repeat my tactics but respond to circumstances in an infinite variety of ways'.

The same principle can be applied to the business world. Richard Pascale puts it well: nothing fails like success. No CEO can reasonably expect that the same business model and strategy will always bring success. Strategists need to look at the underlying assumptions which drive their industry and at the behaviour of their competitors. Taking the opportunity to 'change the rules' can be a source of competitive advantage.

Sun Tzu's ideas are attractive and powerful because they transcend fad and fashion. The broad principles they set out provide a solid base on which to build a strategy.

That said, some modern-day strategists may find the examination of strategy in a militaristic and combative context a little out of place in these more complex, politically correct, win-win times, maintaining that today's companies focus less on attempting to destroy the competition and more on forming an optimal relationship with customers. However, there are plenty of organizations for which the imagery of business as war will seem all too appropriate.

Zeitbite

The wisdom of Sun Tzu

Part of Sun Tzu's appeal is that he can encapsulate his thinking in short, memorable chunks. This, of course, makes him ideal material for corporate presentations! Here are some of his nuggets of wisdom, all drawn from *The Art of War*:

- 'Carefully compare the opposing army with your own, so that you may know where strength is superabundant and where it is deficient.'
- 'All men can see the tactics whereby I conquer, but what none can see is the strategy out of which victory is evolved.'
- 'When the general is weak and without authority; when his orders are not clear and distinct; when there are no fixed duties assigned to officers and men, and the ranks are formed in a slovenly haphazard manner, the result is utter disorganization.'
- 'On which side is discipline most rigorously enforced? ... In which army is there the greater constancy both in reward and punishment? By means of these considerations I can forecast victory or defeat.'
- 'When the common soldiers are too strong and their officers too weak, the result is insubordination. When the officers are too strong and the common soldiers too weak, the result is collapse.'
- 'If soldiers are punished before they have grown attached to you, they will not prove submissive; and, unless submissive, they will be practically useless. If, when the soldiers have become attached to you, punishments are not enforced, they will still be useless. Therefore soldiers must be treated in the first instance with humanity, but kept under control by means of iron discipline. This is a certain road to victory.'
- 'Throw your soldiers into positions whence there is no escape, and they will prefer death to flight. If they will face death, there is nothing they may not achieve.'

- 'You can be sure of succeeding in your attacks if you only attack places which are undefended. You can ensure the safety of your defence if you only hold positions that cannot be attacked.'
- 'Whoever is first in the field and awaits the coming of the enemy will be fresh for the fight; whoever is second in the field and has to hasten to battle will arrive exhausted.'
- 'The captured soldiers should be kindly treated and kept. This is called using the conquered foe to augment one's own strength.'
- 'We cannot enter into alliances until we are acquainted with the designs of our neighbours.'

The author

Sun Tzu is believed to have lived in China around 2500 BC. He wrote *The Art of War* in 13 chapters for Ho Lu, King of Wu, and he was subsequently made a general by the king.

Sources and further reading

Sun Tzu, *The Art of War*, various publishers.
   As Sun Tzu's classic is out of copyright, there are any number of versions available in print. There are also a number of websites containing the full text of the book. For example, try The Gutenberg Project website at http://promo.net/pg/
Dr Foo Check Teck, 1995, *Sun Tzu on Management*, Butterworth-Heinemann, Oxford.
   In this book, Dr Foo, a university lecturer in international business strategy from Singapore, sets out to write the larger book that Sun Tzu himself might have produced, and in so doing he tries to reveal the thinking behind the strategic principles that Sun Tzu propounded. Presented in the form of a 'novel diary', the result is a stunning and, at over 500 pages, a substantial act of imagination that transports the reader back in time to the hut high in the mountains where the general is thought to have spent the last years of his life.

WATTS WACKER & JIM TAYLOR, WITH HOWARD MEANS

The 500 Year Delta

1997

I t doesn't seem that far back in the corporate timeline that change used to happen in bursts, if at all. Occasionally, if you remember, a new CEO would have a rush of blood and personally re-design the business on the back of attending an executive seminar, or perhaps bring in some consultants to help. Senior managers would sigh, brace themselves for a few bumpy months and look forward to a time when life in the company would settle down again. Then, say in the mid- to late eighties, companies realized they would have to flick the change switch onto constant and things would never be quite the same again.

And now, with constant change absorbed as an unquestioned given on most corporate agendas, post-millennial business life is due for another shake-up, say Watts Wacker and Jim Taylor in this gripping and mind-boggling book.

Every 500 years or so, say the authors, civilization encounters a period of change so vast and sweeping that nothing remains the same as before. In *The 500 Year Delta*, they set out to demonstrate that we are now at a turning point in history as pivotal and disruptive as the birth of Christianity, the fall of the Roman Empire, the disintegration of the feudal system, and the Renaissance. Citing hard statistics as well as anecdotal evidence, they argue that we are now seeing the simultaneous collapse of the logical, social and economic assumptions we have lived by for the past 500 years. We are, they say, making the transition from the Age of Reason into a new, chaos-based Age of Access.

And driving this transition, they say, are the two usual suspects, globalization and the impact of technology. People are no longer constrained by ties of blood or geography. They construct their own communities on the internet, on the phone, or in the workplace. The once separate domains of work, leisure and family have converged.

To explore the implications of this transition, Wacker and Taylor draw on the strategies and actions of various forward-looking individuals and fast companies to pinpoint some fundamental practices that people will need to adopt in order to survive the current chaos and to prosper in the new millennium.

These include:

- Gathering information constantly to prepare for decision making at a moment's notice.
- Forgetting process and focusing on outcome, because in a world of increasing complexities, the critical issue is where you want to be, not how you get there.
- Planning around the certainty of uncertainty. Begin by making a list of the five worst things that could happen to your company and career and developing a scenario for each one. Forget the five-year plan; you'll never be able to anticipate accurately a future that is that far away.
- Treating each customer as an individual market. Constantly reinforce the unique value of your product or service in meeting his or her needs.
- Owning ideas not property, and concentrating on hiring individuals who have the power to process information, analyse the interests of consumers and come up with the innovations that create new revenue.
- Expunging the givens that have guided you in the past – the infallibility of reason, loyalty, working the chain of command, relying on precedents, career building tactics – and instead embracing irrationality, self-interest and entrepreneurial impulses.
- Institutionalizing diversity – not because it's politically correct, but because greater diversity makes available the multiple perspectives necessary for instantaneous responses to chaotic circumstances.
- Letting employees make decisions. Open up communication, but control the process. In other words, loosen your grip by controlling risks, not behaviour.
- Practising intelligent disobedience. Break rules to build change, not difference.

Do Taylor and Wacker's ideas amount to much more than hippy-trippy psycho-babble? At a time when for many of us the workplace is relocating from the factory or office to the spare room, and when we are more likely to keep in contact with friends by e-mail rather that over a pint at The King's Arms on a Friday night, it seems possible that they are onto

Zeitbite

Here is a set of quotes drawn from *The 500 Year Delta*. Wise and insightful, or mildly bonkers? You decide.

'Cause has come unhinged from effect.'

'We live increasingly in a world where the givens not only don't hold, but can be impossible to determine.'

'The more you search for causality, the further behind you will fall.'

'Like viruses, we live off organizations without particularly respecting them or even believing in them.'

'No mountain of data about the mass market can predict how one customer will act, because once you parse her at this individual level, you come to understand that she acts out of entirely individual motives.'

'Only by operating at the edge of the extremes, by courting provocation, can a manager inject the information that challenges people to keep thinking about the business in a different way.'

'Until consumers are involved directly in the communication transaction, one-to-many advertisers are shouting, very expensively, into the wind.'

'Perhaps the chief reason that the explosion in information has bred such widespread discontent is that too much information is chasing too few decisions.'

'If you were to be given the choice of being presented with all the assets of the Coca-Cola Company, including the formulas for the drinks but not including the name, or only the name, which would you take?'

'You manage your risk not by pretending it doesn't exist, but by offering authenticity.'

'Learning to swim with chaos requires the recognition that in the Chaos Age you have to operate from self-interest.'

something. Their purpose in any event, they say, is not to be right but rather to make people think and maybe re-examine taken-for-granted assumptions.

Sometimes stimulating, sometimes a tad pretentious, always intriguing, their book certainly achieves that. And given that they number BP, Bank of America, Nike Inc, Barclays and ICL among their consultancy clients, perhaps it won't be too long before Wacker and Taylor find their take on the future of work becoming the new conventional wisdom.

The authors

Watts Wacker is CEO at FirstMatter LLC, a Westport, Connecticut-based consultancy that aims to bring the future to corporations. He can be contacted at watts.wacker@firstmatter.com

Jim Taylor is a lecturer and consultant, and Howard Means is a novelist and editor of *The Washingtonian*.

Sources and further reading

Watts Wacker and Jim Taylor, with Howard Means, 1997, *The 500 Year Delta*, Capstone, Oxford.

Watts Wacker and Jim Taylor, with Howard Means, 2000, *The Visionary's Handbook*, HarperBusiness, New York.

Ryan Mathews and Watts Wacker, 2002, *The Deviants Advantage*, Crown Business Publications, New York.

Ryan Mathews and Watts Wacker, March 2002, 'Deviants, Inc.', *Fast Company*.

MICHAEL J WOLF

The Entertainment Economy

1999

G oing to watch a movie is an experience that can fall into a number of different categories. At one level, it might simply while away a couple of hours on a rainy day in a warm and comfortable environment; at another level, the movie might arouse curiosity or amuse us; at yet another level, a movie can change the way we think or feel about something. In other words, a movie can engage an audience at a number of different levels.

This is not a totally novel concept. In a sense, the behavioural psychologist Abraham Maslow predicted this when he drew up his theory of motivation and stated that people's needs fall into a hierarchy. Basic needs such as food, warmth and shelter are at the bottom, more complex emotional needs in the middle, and 'self actualization' at the top. As each need is satisfied, people move up to the next.

The challenge to businesses is to move their products and services up the hierarchy. Take Starbucks as a shining example; it has created an entire experience out of drinking coffee within an industry that was increasingly commoditized and price-driven.

Michael Wolf founded and heads the media and entertainment practice at Booz-Allen & Hamilton in New York and has spent the last ten years consulting with the media moguls who head up the world's largest entertainment companies.

In *The Entertainment Economy*, he argues that media and entertainment have moved beyond mere culture to become the driving force of the global retail economy. As he puts it, 'there's no business without show business'. In this world where 'entertainment content has become a key differentiator in virtually every aspect of the broader consumer economy', all consumer businesses need to acknowledge the multi-level relationships that entertainment businesses set out to build with their customers. In other words, in a world where businesses compete primarily for the time and attention of customers, content becomes king, and the quality of the experience the clincher.

However, perhaps the most useful insight of this book is that not all businesses will, or should, adopt an entertainment-based approach. As consumers look to satisfy more complex emotional needs, they become increasingly reluctant to waste time on lower-order ones. Wolf argues that retail will split into two paths: one headed towards entertainment venues, the other headed towards convenience. For companies on the latter path, convenience, price and consistent quality rather than entertainment remain the key variables. To buy a regular, no-frills item like a T-shirt, most consumers will go for a low-hassle, low-cost solution, which might involve spending a few minutes in their chosen store. Even better, they increasingly are saving themselves the trouble of going out at all by ordering it over the internet.

This book is a compelling read for anyone who is even remotely interested in the media and entertainment world. Its great strength is that Michael Wolf is a real industry insider who continually engages the reader with examples and stories from across the industry. However, the danger is that the book's conversational style and entertainment-centred focus might mislead people into viewing it as an enjoyable and insightful read rather than a ground-breaking work with the potential to speak to a wider audience. *The Entertainment Economy* has some valid and highly relevant messages for the business world, but the book's lack of charts, tables, graphs, or even any bullet-points means that extracting these messages requires quite a bit of work on the business reader's part.

The author

Michael J Wolf is a senior partner in the New York-based media and entertainment practice at Booz-Allen & Hamilton, a unit that he set up in 1991.

Sources and further reading

Michael J Wolf, 1999, *The Entertainment Economy: The mega-media forces that are shaping our lives*, Random House, New York.

B Joseph Pine II and James H Gilmore, 1999, *The Experience Economy: Goods and Services are no longer enough*, Harvard Business School Press, Boston.

WALT WRISTON

The Twilight of Sovereignty

1992

During his 17-year spell as chairman and CEO of Citicorp/
Citibank, Walter Wriston was regarded by many as the most
influential and technologically aware banker on the planet. He
was in at the ground floor of the creation of the modern wired
economy and, by the time he retired in 1984, Citibank had become the
world's largest bank, with its investment in computers and software
coming in at an astonishing $1.75 billion.

In *The Twilight of Sovereignty: How the Information Revolution is
Transforming Our World*, Wriston set out to address the issues facing
American corporations and the wider world during the 1990s and
beyond.

In the book he argues that, where once the basis for wealth had
moved from land to labour, it is now evolving from labour to information. This, he writes, is transforming the way we live, work, govern and
communicate.

Wriston's central thesis is that information is an unstoppable,
democratizing force. He writes that 'the Information Age is rapidly
giving power to the people ... in a way that only a few years ago seemed
impossible ... Freedom is a virus for which there is no antidote and the
virus is spread on the electronic network.'

The sovereignty whose twilight Wriston refers to in the title of his
book is the supreme power enjoyed by a nation state in regulating the
behaviour of people and corporations within its borders. Such regulation depends on a world of tangibility, where it is relatively straightforward to count, track and tax things. When information is the product,
i.e. something that has no physical existence, states cannot track it or tax
it. States can control what enters and leaves their physical borders, but

Zeitbite

Walt's wisdom

'I've driven through my share of rainstorms, listening to some radio announcer in a windowless room telling me that it's a sunny day.

'During a change in economic climate, the biggest mistake a leader can make is not to recognize it. So never stop looking out the window. Accurately assessing the business cycle is key to your company's success.

'In economic hard times, you have to shift your attention from the top line to the bottom line. Start thinking about profit, rather than revenue. Cash is king, especially when the wind blows. Get back to basics like inventory control, receivables, payables, and cash flow – all of those boring things that people have nearly forgotten about in the new economy. Focus on generating cash, and your company will be positioned to take advantage of opportunities that the cash-strapped can't afford.

'And just remember to recognize when the weather is shifting. Rain or shine – look out.'

From an interview with Walt Wriston in *Fast Company*, May 2001

information will not be restrained. Wriston put it pithily: 'satellites are no respecters of ideology'.

Information, says Wriston, is breaking down the sovereignty of governments and other large bureaucracies. The convergence of computers and telecommunications is destabilizing and decentralizing both power and knowledge. Within the corporation, too, the twilight of sovereignty is near. The immediate and simultaneous availability of data to those at every level of authority within the organization means that, in today's working world, the traditional executive mantra that knowledge is power is also having to change.

A decade on from the publication of *The Twilight of Sovereignty*, Wriston remains a highly relevant read. Despite the bumpy ride that the new economy has had, human intelligence and intellectual resources are now the world's prime capital. His prescience is all the more impressive given that he wrote his book three years before Netscape popularized the world-wide web. Of course, there is no mention in *The Twilight of Sovereignty* of the internet, the world-wide web, cybertraders, and other such commonplace phenomena of today. Though he did not foresee the detail, he certainly got the broad picture correct.

The Twilight of Sovereignty compresses its wisdom into only 192 pages. That said, aside from the occasional memorable line, Wriston's writing style is distinctly pedestrian. The real compensation for the reader is that his thinking never is.

The author

Walter Wriston joined Citibank in 1946, and served as president and CEO for seventeen years until his retirement in 1984. From 1982 to 1989, he was chairman of then-President Ronald Reagan's Economic Policy Advisory Board. *The Twilight of Sovereignty* is his second book; the first – *Risk & Other Four-Letter Words* – was published by Harper & Row in 1986.

Sources and further reading

Walt Wriston, 1992, *The Twilight of Sovereignty: How the Information Revolution is Transforming Our World*, Charles Scribner's Sons, New York.

SHOSHANA ZUBOFF

In the Age of the Smart Machine

1988

ased on research carried out in the US by Shoshana Zuboff during the late 1970s and early 1980s, *In the Age of the Smart Machine* is a real rarity – a technology classic. Zuboff achieves this feat by concentrating less on the technology itself and more on its meaning and potential.

In the Age of the Smart Machine sets out to document the pitfalls and promise of computerized technology in business life. Picking through the book brings out a number of key themes, most of which still have great relevance today. Zuboff, for example, touches on all of the following issues, either explicitly or implicitly:

- Information technologies can transform work at every organizational level by having the potential to give all employees a comprehensive or near-comprehensive view of the entire business. These technologies will surrender knowledge to anyone with the requisite skills. This contrasts with earlier generations of technological advance where the primary impact of new machines was to decrease the complexity of tasks.
- Information technologies can potentially increase the intellectual content of work at all levels. Work involves an ability to understand, respond to, manage, and create value from information. The most effective organizations will be those that achieve a more equitable distribution of knowledge and authority.
- Information technology presents us with a fateful choice: do we use it to continue automation at the risk of robbing workers of gratification and self image, or to empower ordinary working people to make judgements?

- Unlocking the promise of information technology depends on dismantling managerial hierarchies that all too often seek to block the ready flow of information.
- Information technology has the capacity not only to change where knowledge and power reside in the organization; it also changes time. The 'working day' has less meaning in a global village where communication via electronic mail, voice mail, and facsimile transmissions can be sent or received at any time of day or night.
- Paradoxically, as the working day has expanded, so time has contracted. Companies compete on speed, using effective co-ordination of resources to reduce the time needed to develop new products, deliver orders or react to customer requests.
- Even more dramatically, new information technologies offer the possibility of restructuring whole industry sectors. Traditional value-chain structures are fragmenting and reforming. Zuboff predicted the emergence of 'virtual' organizations.
- If a company can replace an employee with a computer programme that does not demand an ever-increasing salary, a pension, cheap mortgage or insurance, the danger is that it will. As a consequence, people can lose their outdated jobs almost overnight and remain unemployable because they lack the variety of skills and mental flexibility to adjust.
- As with the original industrial revolution, there are bound to be winners and losers. For every empowered, delayered, nano-technology worker doing valuable work, there is another who has lost his or her job, and yet another tucked away in a technologically Neanderthal office putting in longer and longer hours doing more of the same work. Are we destined to live in a world where some people are permanently overworked while others are permanently underworked?

Perhaps the most crucial point she raises revolves around how we humans relate to technology. In the final analysis, technology's potential is limited primarily by the power of the human imagination. As B F Skinner once wrote, 'the real question is not whether machines think, but whether men do'.

Zuboff goes further, arguing in a *Scientific American* article that technological capability has galloped ahead of our ability to cope because 'so far, patterns of morality, sociality, and feeling are evolving much more slowly than technology'.

The impact of information technology on organizations over the past 20 years or so has been huge. By enabling the creation of a global

Zuboff on the informated workplace

'The informated workplace, which may no longer be a "place" at all, is an arena through which information circulates, information to which intellective effort is applied. The quality, rather than the quantity, of effort will be the source from which added value is derived. Economists may continue to measure labour productivity as if the entire world of work could be represented adequately by the assembly line, but their measures will be systematically indifferent to what is most valuable in the informated organization. A new division of learning requires another vocabulary – one of colleagues and co-learners, of exploration, experimentation, and innovation. Jobs are comprehensive, tasks are abstractions that depend upon insight and synthesis, and power is a roving force that comes to rest as dictated by function and need. A new vocabulary cannot be invented all at once – it will emerge from the practical action of people struggling to make sense in a new "place" and driven to sever their ties with an industrial logic that has ruled the imaginative life of our century.

'The informated organization is a learning institution, and one of its principal purposes is the expansion of knowledge – not knowledge for its own sake (as in academic pursuit), but knowledge that comes to reside at the core of what it means to be productive. Learning is no longer a separate activity that occurs either before one enters the workplace or in remote classroom settings. Nor is it an activity preserved for a managerial group. The behaviours that define learning and the behaviours that define being productive are one and the same. Learning is not something that requires time out from being engaged in productive activity; learning is the heart of productive activity. To put it simply, learning is the new form of labour.

'The precise contours of a new division of learning will depend upon the business, products, services, and markets that people are engaged in learning about. The empowerment, commitment, and involvement of a wide range of organizational members in self-managing activities means that organizational structures are likely to be both emergent and flexible, changing as members continually learn more about how to organize themselves for learning about their business. However, some significant conceptual issues are raised by the prospect of a new division of learning in the informated organization. The following discussion of these issues does not offer a rigid prescription for practice but suggests the kinds of concrete choices that define an informating strategy.'

Extracted from *In the Age of the Smart Machine*

marketplace, and by decentralizing control and empowering people all along the information chain, technology redefines what is possible for organizations. New computer-based systems dissolve conventions of ownership, design, manufacturing, executive style, and national identity. This has profound implications for organizations.

Perhaps though, based on Zuboff's considerable insights, the most vital question that we need to address is whether, as technology surges further and further ahead, we are still at heart emotional Luddites.

The author

Shoshana Zuboff is a professor at the Harvard Business School. She has written extensively about how computers will affect the future of work.

Sources and further reading

Shoshana Zuboff, 1988, *In the Age of the Smart Machine: The future of work and power*, Basic Books, New York.
Shoshana Zuboff, September 1995, 'The Emperor's New Workplace', *Scientific American*.

CODA:
THE FUTURE OF STRATEGY

'More than at any other time in history, mankind faces a crossroad: one path leads to despair and hopelessness, and the other to total extinction. Let us pray we have the wisdom to choose correctly.'

Woody Allen

There's no real knowing where strategy might be heading over the next few years. As movie mogul Sam Goldwyn once famously said, 'it's difficult to make predictions, especially about the future'. However, there is a growing body of opinion within the strategy field that the world is essentially unpredictable and the future inherently unknowable because events are chaotic in nature.

Chaos theory is a broad body of work that looks at the underlying behaviour of systems, which are governed by simple physical laws, but where events appear to be so unpredictable that they might as well be random. In this sense, 'chaos' does not mean absolute muddle and confusion; it is the study of the complex relationships that underlie the 'everyday' systems that we observe in the real world. In reality, these relationships are non-linear and dynamic, making them extraordinarily complex because a single action can have a host of different effects, causing the surface links between 'cause' and 'effect' to disappear (or be hidden within a more complex system). Moreover, we cannot meaningfully approximate these relationships using the kind of linear assumptions with which we feel comfortable. As James Gleick, the author of *Chaos, Making a New Science*, writes in the prologue of his book:

'Watch two bits of foam flowing side by side at the bottom of a waterfall. What can you guess about how close they were at the top? Nothing. As far as standard physics was concerned, God might just as well have taken all those water molecules under the table and shuffled them personally ... Tiny differences in input [can] quickly become overwhelming differences in output – a phenomenon given the name "sensitive dependence on initial condition." In weather, for example, this translates into what is only half-jokingly known as the Butterfly Effect – the notion that a butterfly stirring the air today in Peking can transform storm systems next month in New York.'

The greatest contribution of chaos theory is the realization that even the simplest systems are now seen to create extraordinarily difficult problems of predictability. This represents nothing less than a paradigm shift because it challenges our implicit assumption that we live in a stable world where instability is the exception.

The truth is that we live in a chaotic universe ruled by entropy, the inexorable tendency towards greater and greater disorder. In these circumstances it is no surprise that long-term planning has been notoriously inaccurate in predicting the future. Indeed, detailed planning systems, and the econometric models that sometimes underlie them, cannot be effective because we simply cannot look with any certainty into the future.

Strategy is adapting by borrowing concepts originating in the sciences, notably both physics and biology. This strategic lens stresses adaptability, flexibility and speed of change rather than static positioning and long-term competitive advantage. It is not just 'running faster' but 'thinking faster' that matters.

Perhaps there are still organizations for which the future is clearly laid out and whose place in the world is assured. But their numbers are declining rapidly – just ask Marconi. For most of us working in or with organizations, the challenge is to throw away the strategic rulebook and focus instead on capturing unanticipated, fleeting opportunities in order to succeed. In traditional strategy, advantage has come from exploiting resources or stable market positions. In future strategy, advantage comes from successfully exploiting these fleeting opportunities.

This will require an organization to have unprecedented levels of flexibility. This in turn is likely to impose psychological and emotional traumas on its employees since there are limits to an individual's ability to respond to rapid external changes. Paradoxically, this increases the importance of maintaining a stable centre, based on a strong set of organizational values.

And for now: stay vigilant

In their book *Profit from the Core* (HBS Press, 2001), Chris Zook and James Allen suggest the following ten questions that management teams should periodically ask themselves about their companies as they find themselves in an almost infinite variety of strategic situations.

1 What is the most tightly defined profitable core of our business, and is it gaining or losing strength?
2 What defines the boundaries of the business that we are competing for, and where are those boundaries going to shift in the future?
3 Are there new competitors currently at the fringe of our business that pose potential longer-term threats to the core?
4 Are we certain that we are achieving the full strategic and operating potential of our core business, the 'hidden value' of the core?
5 What is the full set of potential adjacencies to our core business and possible adjacency moves (single or multiple moves)? Are we looking at these in a planned, logical sequence or piecemeal?
6 What is our point of view on the future of the industry? As a team, do we have consensus? How is this point of view shaping our adjacency strategy and point of arrival?
7 Should major new growth initiatives be pursued inside, next to, or outside the core? How should we decide?
8 Is industry turbulence changing the fundamental source of future competitive advantage? How? Through new models? New segments? New competitors? And what are we monitoring on a regular basis?
9 Are organizational enablers and inhibitors to growth in the right balance for the needed change?
10 What are the guiding strategic principles that should apply consistently to all of our major strategic and operating decisions?

There may well be other key questions that apply to your particular company in your particular industry at this particular time. But being able to address the questions posed by Zook and Allen will put you in a stronger position than most of your competitors.

Good luck!

ANNOTATED BIBLIOGRAPHY

Life, as we know, is rarely neat. So it should surprise nobody that there were a number of books over and above the 50 that comprise the body of *The Ultimate Strategy Library* that came close to being included. Here is an annotated bibliography, arranged alphabetically by author, of 50 more strategy books that deserve at least an honourable mention.

Scott Adams

The Dilbert Principle, HarperCollins, New York, 1996.

Not since the early days of *The Far Side* by Gary Larson has there been a cartoon strip to match Dilbert, a mouthless bespectacled computer nerd whose observations on modern business life are poignant, irreverent and painfully funny. For office dwellers across the world, Dilbert has become an essential part of their lives, a touchstone with reality when the world around them seems to be going crazy.

What is it that makes *The Dilbert Principle* so good? The caustic dramas that unfold around new management trends? The reflection on the absurdity of much of everyday modern business life? Like all truly great cartoons, Dilbert is hard to pin down because it operates on so many levels. It is all these things and much, much more.

If you are not familiar with the work of Scott Adams, sample one of the Dilbert cartoon anthologies (*Build a Better Life by Stealing Office Supplies* is a very good start-point) and you will soon be smitten. If you are already familiar with Dilbert, you almost certainly have this book already.

Douglas F Aldrich

Mastering the Digital Marketplace: Practical strategies for competitiveness in the New Economy, John Wiley, New York, 2000.

In the digital economy, argues Aldrich, there are two key measures of value: time (as in how much time your product or service will save the customer) and content (information, knowledge, or services that provide added value to the customer). He goes on to outline a new business model which he calls the Digital Value Network (DVN), a community of electronically linked business partners that work together to produce value for the customer as the customer defines it, and offers strategies for creating and sustaining it.

Peter L Bernstein

Against the Gods, John Wiley, New York, 1996.

Peter Bernstein argues that the notion of bringing risk under control is one of the core ideas that separates modern times from the past. This lucid and fascinating book tells the story of risk from its earliest beginnings before moving onto an examination of risk in the economy at large and the financial markets particularly. Makes a complex subject very accessible.

Susan Blackmore

The Meme Machine, Oxford University Press, Oxford, 1999.

Once humans learned to receive, copy and retransmit memes – in essence a captivating idea, behaviour, or skill that can be transferred from one person to another by imitation – the rest, says Blackmore, is a foregone conclusion. Memetic competition shapes our minds and culture, just as natural selection has shaped our physical evolution. But why should this matter to us and to the organizations we work for? Well for a start, it explains why the sexual adventures of an errant senior manager would grip the corporate imagination more than the latest set of financial figures. Blackmore explores her subject with great panache. Some readers who like to explore both sides of an argument before making up their own minds may find her sure-footed advocacy a little overpowering, but for the rest of us *The Meme Machine* is a riveting and provocative read.

Robin Bloor

The Electronic B@zaar, Nicholas Brealey, London, 2000.

Bloor's mix of leading-edge IT analysis, historical perspective, and a sound grasp of economic principles makes for an informative and entertaining account of the new economic landscape. *The Electronic B@zaar* occasionally reads as though it has been put through some kind of Tom Peters style-writer software, but nonetheless the book is a compelling call-to-arms for anybody seeking practical tips about making the transition from bricks-and-mortar to successful e-business.

Alan Burton-Jones

Knowledge Capitalism, Oxford University Press, Oxford, 1999.

Burton-Jones marshals an impressive range of evidence in this closely argued exploration of how the shift to a knowledge-based economy is redefining the shape and nature of organizations. He also describes the emergence of a new breed of capitalist, one dependent on knowledge rather than physical resources. There are plenty of easier reads about the knowledge economy on the market, but those looking for substance rather than eye-catching glibness will be pleased to find in *Knowledge Capitalism* a book that provides frequent moments of insight without ever compromising *gravitas*.

Alfred Chandler

The Visible Hand: The Managerial Revolution in American Business, Harvard University Press, Boston, 1977.

Chandler argues that modern business emerged when the growing volume of economic activities made administrative coordination more efficient than market coordination. Once this happened, establishing a managerial hierarchy became a prerequisite for realizing the advantages of coordinating multiple units within a single enterprise.

Andrew Campbell and Michael Goold

Synergy, Capstone, Oxford, 1998.

Subtitled *Why links between business units often fail and how to make them work*, this is an insightful and penetrating guide to how and under what circumstances a business portfolio can be worth more than the sum of its parts. Campbell and Goold describe synergy as 'the strategist's holy grail'. If you can get the disparate elements of the organization to work together, they maintain there is an opportunity to create more value without using more resources. They outline six types of synergy, and then go on to explain why synergy can sometimes be difficult to achieve, how to assess the potential benefits, when and how parent companies should intervene to create synergy, the pros and cons of synergy and how to evaluate the success of synergy interventions.

James Creelman

Building and Implementing a Balanced Scorecard, Business Intelligence, 1998.

It is now around five years since Robert Kaplan and David Norton first wrote about the Balanced Scorecard in a *Harvard Business Review* article. For anybody unfamiliar with the concept, the Balanced Scorecard translates an organization's mission and strategy into a comprehensive set of performance measures that provides the framework for a strategic measurement and management system. While the Scorecard's originators have produced a number of books and articles developing and extending the concept, they have been less convincing on some of the practical challenges and issues involved in implementing a Scorecard within an organization. This informative and highly readable report fills that gap admirably, containing as it does instructive case studies, informed and clear-eyed commentary on the benefits and difficulties associated with putting a Scorecard in place, plus regular summaries. The report is not cheap but any company planning to build and implement its own Scorecard would soon recoup the outlay on this report through time saved and mistakes avoided.

Stan Davis and Christopher Meyer

Future Wealth, Harvard Business School Press, Boston, 2000.

In *Future Wealth* – described as the companion volume to the authors' best-selling book *Blur* – Davis and Meyer identify three major consequences of the newly connected economy: risk as opportunity, not only as threat; the growing efficiency of financial markets for human capital; and the need for new forms of social capital.

They go on to explain why they think we are headed toward a new stage of economic development in which 'human and intellectual capital [is] the most highly valued resource'.

Peter Drucker

The Practice of Management, Harper & Row, 1954.
A book of huge range and continuing relevance – the first to explore the concept of Management by Objectives.

Evan Dudik

Strategic Renaissance, Amacom, New York, 2000.
Dudik takes a complex systems approach to strategy, suggesting that the organization needs to understand the level of uncertainty of the future environment, while at the same time needing to create itself as a complex adaptive system in order to deal with uncertainty. An excellent (and lucid) exploration of what organizations must do to thrive in a complex business world.

Jaclyn Easton

StrikingitRich.com, McGraw-Hill, New York, 1999.
Subtitled *Profiles of 23 incredibly successful companies you've probably never heard of,* Jaclyn Easton's rigorously researched and extremely readable book proves that websites don't have to be high-profile extravaganzas to make serious money. The sites demonstrate that it is perfectly possible for a website to achieve a profit quickly if an idea is well conceived and executed and if start-up costs are managed tightly.

Gerard Egan

Working the Shadow Side, Jossey Bass, San Francisco, 1994.
To uncover the *hidden dimension* or *shadow side* of organizational culture demands great honesty, courage and openness in an organization. It can also be a necessity of business survival as Gerard Egan, professor of psychology at Loyola University of Chicago, points out in his book. Managers, he says, are increasingly being forced into the role

of managing chaos and change. The best managers are always looking for ways to become more adept at dealing with the shadow side of the organization – the unspoken, unacknowledged, behind-the-scenes stuff that stands in the way of getting things done efficiently, or even getting things done at all. In today's organizational and business climate, becoming skilled at behind-the-scenes management is not an amenity but a necessity. Failure to deal with the shadow side of change can lead to failure of the business itself.

Malcolm Gladwell

The Tipping Point: How little things can make a big difference, Little Brown, New York, 2000.

Why do some minority tastes remain strictly minority, while others extend into the mainstream? *The Tipping Point* is a well-written and racy exploration of what lies behind the point when a small fad acquires critical mass and takes off. It's very readable but the central idea isn't really enough to sustain a whole book – no surprise then to discover that it began its life as a long article in *New Yorker* magazine.

Robert Heller

In Search of European Excellence, HarperCollins Business, New York, 1997.

With a nod to the Peters and Waterman classic, Heller sets out to identify the key strategies with which Europe's most successful companies are beating their competition. When he looked at the state of European business, he found that Europe's old reactionaries are still in the majority, but that their ascendancy is rapidly draining away as new leaders act decisively in ten arenas of corporate renaissance. These include devolving leadership; driving radical change; reshaping culture; keeping the competitive edge; and achieving total management quality. In each area, Heller gives convincing examples of European companies that have made wholehearted efforts to change. As ever with a book that draws on a large number of case studies, one or two of the companies praised have slipped from grace in recent times. This does not undermine Heller's basic thesis but it does demonstrate how tough it is to hold onto industry leadership once attained.

Eric Hobsbawm

The New Century, Little Brown, New York, 2000.
    In which the pre-eminent historian (you won't find a better account of the twentieth century than his *Age of Extremes*) offers his analysis of the current state of the world. Although the scope of this book goes much wider than the new economy, there's one chapter in particular – called 'The Global Village' – that offers a lucid, cool-headed and reasoned assessment of the global economy. It's a much-needed antidote to the starry-eyed hyperbole that seems to dominate the globalization debate.

Will Hutton and Anthony Giddens

On the Edge, Jonathan Cape, London, 2000.
    On the Edge draws together ten original contributions by leading thinkers like Paul Volcker, Manuel Castells, Arlie Russell Hochschild and George Soros. The overall conclusion seems to be that global capitalism does have huge potential for good but is just as likely to create a set of consequences that most of us would rather avoid. Co-author and Work Foundation boss Will Hutton describes global capitalism as 'precarious and potentially dangerous'. An important book that takes a clear-eyed view of its subject.

Elliott Jaques

Requisite Organization, Cason Hall, Massachusetts, 1996.
    Based on Jaques's latest research, this is a thorough revision of the original book published in 1989. For over 50 years, Jaques has consistently advocated the need for a scientific approach to understanding work systems. He argues that there is a 'widespread, almost universal, under-estimation of the impact of organization on how we go about our business'. He believes, for example, that rapid change in people's behaviour is achieved less through altering their psychological make-up and more by revising organizational structures and managerial leading practices.
    Requisite Organization challenges many current assumptions about effective organizations, particularly in the field of hierarchy – of which Jaques is a fan.

Some may find his theories indigestible, but for those who persist there is a wealth of challenging material that undermines much conventional organizational wisdom.

Larry Kahaner

Competitive Intelligence, Simon and Schuster, New York, 1996.
In a world of rapid technological change where new and sometimes surprising competitors can suddenly appear, a company's success will increasingly depend on how effectively it can gather, analyse and use information. According to Kahaner, companies that can turn raw information into powerful intelligence will 'build market share, launch new products, increase profits and destroy competitors'. Using a series of case studies, this book provides a useful overview of a number of intelligence-gathering techniques, even if some of them – benchmarking, for example – are pretty familiar by now. An informative book, nonetheless, that illustrates how much information is either a matter of public record or is readily and legally accessible.

Robert Kanigel

The One Best Way, Little Brown, New York, 1997.
The One Best Way is an illuminating biography of Frederick W Taylor, the efficiency expert and 'the father of scientific management'. Although he lived through little of it – he died in 1915, aged 59 – Taylor's influence on the twentieth century is unquestionable. Peter Drucker, for example, rates him alongside Freud and Darwin as a maker of the modern world. And despite its critics, Taylorism lives on, whether in the form of reengineering (a direct descendant of scientific management), the continuing debate about the de-skilling of jobs, or the global standardization of companies like McDonald's. At 570 pages, the book is definitely top-heavy with detail. However, as an introduction to arguably the world's first management consultant, it makes fascinating reading.

Susanne Kelly and Mary Ann Allison

The Complexity Advantage, McGraw Hill, New York, 1999.
This book argues that anybody operating in a business world growing ever more complex would benefit from an understanding of

complexity theory. *The Complexity Advantage* represents a serious and sustained attempt to incorporate complexity principles and methodologies into business thinking. The more general reader may initially be baffled by some of the terminology but persistence will pay off.

Kevin Kelly

Out of Control: The new biology of machines, Addison Wesley Inc., New York, 1994.

This is a sprawling, provocative, and massive (at over 600 pages) exploration of the organic nature of human-made systems. It's crammed with original insights all clustered around Kelly's view that our technological future is headed toward a neo-biological civilization. There are those who would argue that this is Kelly's true masterpiece.

Art Kleiner

The Age of Heretics, Nicholas Brealey Publishing, London, 1996.

'Corporate heretics' are those people within an organization who believe in a truth that contradicts the conventional wisdom of their time. Many of them see their ideas ignored or their efforts undermined. Nonetheless, their ideas eventually take root.

Kleiner describes the impact on the history of post-war business of a succession of these maverick, independent-thinking individuals. He goes on to show how the heretical ideas of the 1950s, 1960s and 1970s – self-managed teams, customer focus, scenario planning and so on – have now been absorbed into mainstream corporate thinking. Perhaps his conclusion is overly upbeat. Are today's organizations really 'beginning to understand how much there is to learn from dissent'? Is life really that much easier for heretics currently working for organizations who believe themselves to be infallible?

Richard Koch

The 80/20 Principle, Nicholas Brealey Publishing, London, 1997.

Richard Koch has taken the so-called Pareto Effect – that 80% of results flow from just 20% of the causes – and applied it to individuals, organizations and society at large. His research into business, for example, shows that it is not unusual for 20% of products to generate 80%

206 • The Ultimate Strategy Library

of sales, or for 20% of customers to account for 80% of a company's business. Koch suggests that individuals and organizations can achieve much more with much less effort, and sets out a number of strategies that achieve the desired impact.

Andy Law

Open Minds, Orion, London, 1998.

St Luke's is a high-profile London-based advertising agency and Andy Law has been the company's iconoclastic chairman since 1995. Owned entirely by its employees, all physical resources – offices, PCs etc. – in the company are shared, and there is little hierarchy. Employees are involved in almost all decisions, including setting their own pay rises. Whether the model developed at St Luke's has the resilience to cope with a down-turn in its business fortunes (the company has enjoyed continuous growth since its creation) remains to be seen. In the meantime, *Open Minds* makes a compelling case study, describing and explaining as it does the business practices and philosophy behind this fascinating company.

Charles Leadbeater

Living on Thin Air, Penguin, London, 1999.

In *Living on Thin Air*, Leadbeater argues that society will need to be organized around the creation of knowledge capital and social capital, rather than simply being dominated by the power of financial capital. He draws on research in California, Japan, Germany and the Far East to show how his provocative manifesto might be achieved. He puts over his ideas in a highly informative and accessible way and argues his case well, although some readers may feel that his take on the future is more optimistic than the facts seem to justify.

Jordan Lewis

Trusted Partners, Free Press, New York, 1999.

Mergers and alliances on an ever-grander scale are a feature of the global economy. *Trusted Partners* describes how to build trust between organizations that are forging alliances of various types with other companies, and explores how interpersonal relationships are a critical element of that. Drawing on experience built over four decades of working with some of the world's leading companies, Lewis goes well beyond theoretical analysis of the nature of trust between corporate 'rivals' to lay out some practical and eminently sensible steps involved in building and maintaining trust.

Marshall McLuhan

Understanding Media, Sphere, London, 1964.

Marshall McLuhan's investigation into the state of the then emerging mass media is an exuberant, provocative and scatter-gun piece of work. Much of the challenge he made to sixties' sensibilities and assumptions about how and what we communicate still holds good. *Understanding Media* reads like a work in progress that connects to the modern business world in the same way that HG Wells linked to the Apollo moon landings.

Henry Mintzberg with JB Quinn

The Strategy Process, Prentice-Hall, Harlow, various editions since 1988.

There is no one best definition of strategy in Mintzberg's view. Believing that explicit recognition of multiple definitions can help people to manoeuvre through this difficult field, he provides five views of strategy in this book: Strategy as Plan; Strategy as Ploy; Strategy as Pattern; Strategy as Position; and Strategy as Perspective.

James F Moore

The Death of Competition, HarperCollins, New York, 1996.

Business as ecosystem – Moore explores the biological metaphor in great detail and with considerable insight. One of the first, and arguably the best, exploration of leadership and strategy in a future that Moore envisions will be characterized by organized chaos.

Rosabeth Moss Kanter

World Class: Thriving locally in the global economy, Simon and Schuster, New York, 1995.

Professor Moss Kanter tackles big issues in this book: globalization, the future of capitalism, communitarianism, xenophobia, and cultural imperialism. It is a disquieting book – her world is one in which the new colonialism will be brought about by a techno-elite. When she does stop to consider the human side to all this, it is to conclude that sensible xenophobes should see the error of their ways and realize that globalization can only do them good. This is an important book because it comes from a woman who has access to very good data indeed, a woman who ought to know. But if her reading of the rise of the new world class is accurate, this is also a very scary book. The global economy promises global dystopia.

Burt Nanus

Visionary Leadership, Jossey Bass, San Francisco, 1992.

Nanus describes why he believes vision is a critical component of effective leadership, and goes on to set out a step-by-step process for creating and implementing a new sense of direction for the organization. This doesn't imply that coming up with a vision should be treated as a one-off exercise – Nanus describes it as 'running a race with no end'.

Kenichi Ohmae

The Invisible Continent, HarperBusiness, New York, 2000.

According to Ohmae, the invisible continent is the world in which businesses now operate, which is like a new, just-discovered continent. The invisible continent has dimensions: the Visible Dimension – physical things to buy and make; the Borderless World – inevitable globalization; the Cyber Dimension – the internet, mobile phones; and the Dimension of High Multiples.

Nils-Göran Olve, Jan Roy and Magnus Wetter

Performance Drivers, John Wiley, New York, 1999.

Subtitled 'a practical guide to using the balanced scorecard', this book gives the reader a step-by-step method to introducing the balanced scorecard into an organization. The book is jam-packed with practical tips and helpful case studies.

Richard Pascale, Mark Milleman and Linda Gioja

Surfing the Edge of Chaos, Texere Publishing, London, 2000.
This book explores how today's business laws have parallels in the laws of nature: evolution creates survivors, genetic mixing breeds stronger descendants, moving too far from core values results in chaos. A bit like Richard Dawkins's *The Selfish Gene*, this book blends scientific information with social comment and history.

Tess Read, Callum Chace and Simon Rowe

The Internet Start-Up Bible, Random House, New York, 2000.
The Internet Start-Up Bible is an accessible, well-written guide about how to plan, research, fund, market and implement a successful internet-based business model. The authors take the logical and too often neglected step of applying the same success criteria to dot-com business start-ups as to traditional ventures. Detailed chapters on business planning and attracting venture capital are followed by sections on various aspects of starting up an internet business – technology, design, marketing and launch – before concluding with business growth and flotation. The book is crammed with useful case studies, extensive links and contact addresses and running quotes from business gurus and key books.

Angus Reid

Shakedown: How the new economy is changing our lives, Doubleday Publishing, New York, 1997.
As chairman and CEO of the Angus Reid Group Inc., a leading Canadian polling firms, Angus Reid has been close to the dreams and aspirations of the Canadian people for close to 20 years. In *Shakedown*, he describes how three major discontinuities are converging to change the shape of Canadian society for ever. The combination of technological change, globalization and the ageing of the population has meant the end of the 'spend and share era' of national prosperity and optimism that characterized Canada from the 1960s to the 1980s, and the beginning of a new uncertainty era, which Reid christens the 'sink or swim' era.

The power of this book is in the detail; how these changes are affecting every aspect of Canadian life today and how they will shape the future. Although the book is written for Canadians, its message is universal and is one that we can all readily identify with.

Gill Ringland

Scenario Planning, Wiley, New York, 1998.

Gill Ringland, ICL's group executive with responsibility for strategy, adds her contribution to the plethora of books published about scenario planning. It gives a nuts-and-bolts account of ICL's experience of building scenarios, as well as drawing on examples from the likes of British Airways and United Distillers. As such, it should appeal to its target audience of managers who have not come across the idea in any detail before.

Harriet Rubin

Soloing: Reaching life's Everest, Random House, New York, 1999.

Few of us can aspire to the heights of the people Rubin quotes, who retreat to stunning locations to think and turn down all but the most fascinating jobs. That said, it's hard not to like this book. It is crammed with practical ideas, unconventional wisdom and handy hints. And who, apart from the worst cynics among us, can resist anyone who insists that we must learn our livings? Maybe Rubin is right. Perhaps we can all arrive at the point where we 'get so good at doing only what [we] love that work feels like play'.

Evan Schwartz

Digital Darwinism, Penguin, London, 1999.

A book title that brings together two of the biggest managerial buzzwords of recent times exerts a certain fascination. According to Schwartz, in an interview published on Amazon.com, *Digital Darwinism* is 'a different way of looking at the web economy and how it's co-evolving with the larger business world around it. It's a way of looking at the web as an ecosystem, where the players are scrounging for money and are competing and co-operating with each other as if they were a species in a natural environment.' This is a fascinating premise and one which merits rather more depth than Schwartz brings to the topic. There is a 17-page introduction entitled 'Frenetic Evolution' in which he notes some interesting parallels between Darwin's theory of evolution and the on-line world. But he goes no further in substantive terms. There are a few links made to what lies at the heart of Digital Darwinism, namely 'seven breakthrough strategies for surviving in the cut-throat web economy', but occasional allusions to 'survival guides' don't constitute the grand theory that Schwartz seems to promise at the outset. The irony is that the seven strategies themselves are a neat encapsulation of what a business – be it an internet start-up or a bricks-and-mortar offshoot – should be doing to achieve web success.

John Seely Brown and Paul Duguid

The Social Life of Information, Harvard Business School Press, Boston, 2000.
    The authors put forward a convincing and eloquent argument that human sociability needs to play an important role in the digital world. They explore the importance of placing information in a social context, highlighting the dangers inherent in separating, in their words, 'text from context'. Their conclusion that the digital world stills needs a human heart at its centre is both plausible and uplifting.

Patricia Seybold

Customers.com, Random House, New York, 1998.
    Customers.com offers practical and implementable advice based on the sound premise that any e-commerce initiative has to begin with the customer. The book contains some instructive case studies about how companies like Hertz, PhotoDisc, National Semiconductor and Wells Fargo are using the internet successfully. Shelfloads of books have now been written on this theme but what sets *Customers.com* apart is Seybold's talent for communicating her 20 years of experience in the technology industry in an accessible and no-nonsense writing style.

Alfred Sloan

My Years with General Motors, Doubleday, New York, 1963.
    In a career spanning over half a century with General Motors, Alfred Sloan held a succession of top management roles, culminat-

ing in him becoming honorary chairman from 1956 until his death in 1966. He is a legendary business figure, and many people credit him with creating a new business form – the multi-divisional, decentralized company. He also changed the world of management forever by vesting real responsibility in his senior managers; before Sloan, managers were rarely anything more than glorified supervisors.

In his book, *My Years with General Motors*, Sloan sets out how he achieved this transformation. By rights, the book should be a gripping read; in the event, it is a turgid and highly selective account, lacking drama and human interest. Any researcher needing to gain an insight into the evolution of business strategy during the first half of the twentieth century should probably read this book. But be warned, it will be duty rather than pleasure that gets you through, with only the very occasional insight to sustain the exercise.

Adrian J Slywotzky, David J Morrison, Ted Moser, Kevin A Mundt and James A Quella

Profit Patterns, John Wiley, New York, 1999.

In *Profit Patterns*, the authors introduce pattern thinking as a means of enabling managers to envision opportunities and design winning strategies ahead of the competition. 'Like the best chess players,' they write, 'masters of business pattern recognition, instead of seeing chaos, know how to identify the strategic picture unfolding within the complexity and discover the pattern behind it all'. The book describes a set of 30 patterns that have occurred in industry after industry, shifting billions of pounds in market value from those who 'missed' them to those who 'mastered' them. Company case studies that feature in the book include Dell, Microsoft and Amazon. Not an easy read particularly, but one that rewards attention.

Thomas A Stewart

The Wealth of Knowledge, Nicholas Brealey, London, 2001.

Stewart follows up his best-selling *Intellectual Capital* (see above) by looking at how to apply the concept to managing knowledge assets and thereby gaining competitive edge. A knowledge economy 'bible' in the making.

Alvin Toffler

Future Shock, Bantam, New York, 1970.
Over three decades ago, Toffler anticipated the waves of anxiety that the technological revolution would engender in this ground-breaking exploration of what happens to people and society when overwhelmed by change.

Kees van der Heijden

Scenarios: The art of strategic conversation, Wiley, New York, 1996.
Van der Heijden, a former head of Shell's Business Environment Division, takes as his starting point a belief that uncertainty 'has the effect of moving the key to success from "the optimal strategy" to the "most skilful strategic process".' After setting out the principles of scenario planning, he moves onto a highly practical section discussing how to help a management team broaden its views and think more strategically about the future.

Watts Wacker and Jim Taylor, with Howard Means

The Visionary's Handbook, HarperBusiness, New York, 2000.
In this gripping and mind-boggling book, the authors advise us to forget constant change, and embrace what they call 'constant paradox' – a continuous collision of opposites that will affect us and the terms of our business and personal lives every moment we are alive. They identify nine paradoxes in all, covering everything from value and time to competition, action, leadership and leisure.

Articles (most recent first)

'There Is No Alternative to … ', *Fast Company*, July 2002.
How do you develop strategy in an uncertain economy? Meet TINA: There Is No Alternative. First, Royal Dutch/Shell pioneered the system of scenario planning to anticipate dramatic changes in the world. But, writes Ian Wylie, when everything starts to change, the way to do planning is to focus on things that don't change.

'Can C K Prahalad Pass the Test?', *Fast Company*, August 2001.
  Can C K build a company around the principles that he has been teaching other high-powered leaders?
'A scary Swiss meltdown', *The Economist*, 21 July 2001.
  How a dud strategy brought a solid company to the brink of bankruptcy.
Leslie P Willcocks and Robert Plant, 'Pathways to E-Business Leadership: Getting From Bricks to Clicks', *Sloan Management Review*, Spring 2001.
'Change Is Sweet', *Fast Company*, June 2001.
  When is a Net strategy more than just a Net strategy?
'Over the counter e-commerce', *The Economist*, 26 May 2001.
'While Welch waited', *The Economist*, 19 May 2001.
  First in a series of case studies of how big, established companies are developing their e-business strategies.
Michael Porter, 'Strategy and the Internet', *Harvard Business Review*, March 2001.
'Strategy Rules', *Fast Company*, January 2001.
'The rise of the infomediary', *The Economist*, 26 June 1999.
  The internet is producing a string of racy new business models.
'A price on the priceless', *The Economist*, 26 June 1999.
  Companies know that their competitive advantage lies increasingly in knowledge and ideas. But what are the ideas worth?
Amory B Lovins, L Hunter Lovins and Paul Hawken, 'A Road Map for Natural Capitalism', *Harvard Business Review*, May/June 1999.
John Hagel III and Marc Singer, 'Unbundling the Corporation', *Harvard Business Review*, March/April 1999.
'Internet economics', *The Economist*, 12 December 1998.
  Some companies succeed in the network economy, others don't. Why?
John S Hammond, Ralph L Keeney and Howard Raiffa, 'The Hidden Traps in Decision Making', *Harvard Business Review*, September/October 1998.
Nigel Nicholson, 'How Hardwired is Human Behaviour', *Harvard Business Review*, July/August 1998.
B Joseph Pine II and James H Gilmore, 'Welcome to the Experience Economy', *Harvard Business Review*, July/August 1998.
'Business strategy: past, present and future', *The Economist*, 11 July 1998.
'Making strategy', *The Economist*, 1 March 1997.

W Chan Kim and Renée Mauborgne, 'Value Innovation: the Strategic Logic of High Growth', *Harvard Business Review*, January/February 1997.

Research conducted by Kim and Mauborgne suggests that successful companies are most often those that re-invent the 'rules of the game' in their industries. By changing the dimensions of an industry they can both serve customers better and save costs in doing so.

Michael Porter, 'What is strategy', *Harvard Business Review*, November/December 1996.

James C Collins and Jerry I Porras, 'Building Your Company's Vision', *Harvard Business Review*, September/October 1996.

Christopher A Bartlett and Sumantra Ghoshal, 'Changing the Role of Top Management: Beyond Systems to People', *Harvard Business Review*, May/June 1995.

John P Kotter, 'Leading Change: Why Transformation Efforts Fail', *Harvard Business Review*, March/April 1995.

John Kotter watched more than 100 companies try to remake themselves better than their competitors. Their efforts have gone under many banners: total quality management, reengineering, right-sizing, restructuring, cultural change, and turnarounds. In almost every case, the goal has been the same: to cope with a new, more challenging market by changing how business is conducted. A few of these efforts have been very successful. A few have been utter failures. Most fall somewhere in between, with a distinct tilt toward the lower end of the scale. In this well-known article, the author discusses the lessons that can be learnt.

Christopher A Bartlett and Sumantra Ghoshal, 'Changing the Role of Top Management: Beyond Structure to Processes', *Harvard Business Review*, January/February 1995.

Christopher A Bartlett and Sumantra Ghoshal, 'Changing the Role of Top Management: Beyond Strategy to Purpose, *Harvard Business Review*, November/December 1994.

'The Vision Thing', *The Economist*, September 1994.

Henry Mintzberg, 'The fall and rise of strategic planning', *Harvard Business Review*, January/February 1994.

'Business as War', *Fast Company*, November 1993.

Business in the new economy is a civilized version of war. Companies, not countries, are battlefield rivals.

Robert S Kaplan and David P Norton, 'Putting the Balanced Scorecard to Work', *Harvard Business Review*, September/October 1993.

Michael Treacy and Fred Wiersema, 'Customer Intimacy and Other Value Disciplines', *Harvard Business Review*, January/February 1993.
Michael Treacy and Fred Wiersema outline three basic value disciplines that companies can use to deliver superior value to customers and establish market leadership; operational excellence, customer intimacy and product innovation.
Ralph Stayer, 'How I learned to let my workers lead', *Harvard Business Review*, November/December 1990.
Henry Mintzberg, 'Crafting Strategy', *Harvard Business Review*, July/August 1987.

Journals, magazines and websites

For readers wanting to keep up to date with developments in the strategy field, the following list of publications and websites are worth dipping into on a regular basis.

The Balanced Scorecard Collaborative

Website for a professional services firm founded by Robert Kaplan and David Norton. www.bscol.com

Balanced Scorecard.com

An on-line community that aims to improve understanding of balanced scorecard implementations in both industry and the not-for-profit sector. Some good links. www.balancedscorecard.com

Business Intelligence

Publisher of some solid but very expensive reports (typically around £600 a copy). Website carries some useful free material though. www.business-intelligence.co.uk/

Centre for Business Innovation

Site managed by consultants Ernst and Young – quality of content varies but occasionally provokes thought. www.businessinnovation.ey.com

The Economist

The best single source of information about what is happening in the world. A mainstream publication but one that will take on some big topics from time to time, and one whose take on the new economy is invariably insightful and clear-eyed. www.economist.com

Fast Company

The magazine is monthly and has been an essential read since it started up in 1996. Of late though, the content – whilst still excellent – has been swamped by increasing volumes of advertising. The companion website is just about the best free site around on the future world of work (it also carries material not found in the magazine). www.fastcompany.com/home.html

Financial Times

Of all the dailies, the *Financial Times* provides the best in-depth coverage of strategy-related issues. Well worth keeping an eye out for their occasional Information Technology surveys. www.ft.com

Harvard Business Review

The most authoritative business monthly on the block. It has tended in the past to be more mainstream than truly groundbreaking in its coverage of business issues. That said, *HBR* has responded well to the challenge to traditional business thinking posed by the new economy, and recent issues have generally contained two or three relevant articles. Also, if you are interested in getting the lowdown on forthcoming books from Harvard's publishing wing several months before publication, the magazine consistently trails major books with articles from the authors. The website provides an overview of the contents of the magazine – no free articles but the executive summaries are there and they are often all you need. www.hbsp.harvard.edu/home.html

Internet Business

Just about the best of the recent flurry of new monthlies about doing business on the internet. Informative mix of case studies, interviews, book extracts, and topical news stories.

Journal of Business Strategies

http://COBA.SHSU.edu/jbs/

Knowledge Management

Magazine aimed at knowledge management professionals. The website carries some useful free material. www.kmmag.co.uk

McKinsey Quarterly

Authoritative on-line journal containing many features and article on strategic issues. www.mckinsey.com/

New Scientist

Important science and technology stories will often appear here first. *New Scientist* also gives good coverage to emerging thinking in the scientific community. www.newscientist.com

Red Herring

A monthly magazine that looks at the companies and trends that are shaping the business of technology. Occasionally prone to obsess about the technology itself rather than the impact of the technology. www.redherring.com

Sloan Management Review

The management journal of the Massachusetts Institute of Technology (MIT). Published quarterly, it features articles by some of the world's leading strategic thinkers, and has a genuinely global range. www.smr.mit.edu/

Strategy & Business

Authoritative quarterly journal. www.strategy-business.com/

Think Tanks

Good start-point for exploring all the UK's major think tanks. www.demos.co.uk/linkuk.htm

Wired magazine

Monthly American magazine that is good at picking up trends about six months before they become trends. www.wired.com/wired/

World Future Society

Not-for-profit educational and scientific organization that explores how social and technological developments are shaping the future. www.wfs.org

GLOSSARY OF STRATEGY TERMS

Like many other business subjects, the theory and practice of strategy has a language of its own. Here is a selective glossary of some of the key terms, key concepts and key thinkers associated with the subject.

Activity-based management – looks at the efficiency and effectiveness of delivering products and services to customers by analysing the primary business processes that enable key customer needs to be met. This customer perspective breaks down the traditional functional silos since business processes are, by and large, activities that are linked *across* functional boundaries.

Adhocracy – a non-bureaucratic networked organization with a highly organic organizational design.

Affiliate marketing – pioneered by the likes of Amazon and CDNow; anybody with a website can sign up with them as a sales affiliate and receive a commission (typically 5%-15%) for any sales that are channelled through the affiliate site.

Architecture – the term used by John Kay in his book *Foundations of Corporate Success* (1993) to describe a system of relationships within an organization, or between an organization and its employees, suppliers and customers, or all of them.

Balanced scorecard – a concept developed by Robert S Kaplan and David P Norton of the Harvard Business School, which supplements traditional financial performance measures with customer, internal business process, and innovation and learning measures. However, the balanced scorecard goes beyond the use of key performance indicators because it specifically integrates accounting and financial information into a management system that focuses the entire organization on implementing its long-term strategy.

Benchmarking – the process of comparing one set of measurements with another set drawn from a source that represents best practice in its field.

Bricks and mortar – companies that use traditional methods of selling and distributing products.

Business strategy – concerned with market positioning and segmentation, matching business structures, following through cost leadership, differentiation and specialization strategies at SBU level.

Business process re-design – involves changing both organizational structure and processes to ensure that future customer needs can be anticipated and fulfilled in the most cost-effective manner. It should not be confused with crude cost-cutting exercises (such as downsizing), although many organizations have used both approaches simultaneously, with the result that the value of process redesign has been permanently tarnished in the eyes of many managers.

Choiceboards – interactive, on-line systems that let people design their own products from a menu of attributes, prices and delivery options.

Clusters – critical masses in one place of linked industries that enjoy a high level of success in their particular field. Famous examples are Silicon Valley and Hollywood, but clusters can be found everywhere. According to Michael Porter, clusters can affect competition in three ways:
- by increasing the productivity of companies based in the area;
- by driving the direction and speed of innovation in their field; and
- by stimulating the formation of new businesses within the cluster.

Communities of practice – groups that form within an organization, typically of their own accord, where members are drawn to one another by a common set of needs that may be both professional and social. Compared to project teams, communities of practice are voluntary, longer-lived, have no specific deliverable, and are responsible only to themselves. Because they are free of formal strictures and hierarchy within an organization, they can be viewed as subversive.

Competitive advantage – John Kay, following in the footsteps of Michael Porter, defines competitive advantage as 'the application of distinctive capability to a specific marketplace differentiating an organization from its competitors and allowing it to achieve above-average returns in that market'.

Competitive convergence – what happens when companies are drawn towards imitation and homogeneity. The result is often static or declining prices and downward pressures on costs that compromise companies' ability to invest in the business in the long term.

Competitive intelligence – in a world of rapid technological change where new and sometimes surprising competitors can suddenly appear, a company's success will increasingly depend on how effectively it can gather, analyse and use information. According to Larry Kahaner, author of a book on the subject, companies that can turn raw information into powerful intelligence will 'build market share, launch new products, increase profits and destroy competitors'.

Confusion marketing – a method used by some businesses to deny customers the means of making an informed choice through swamping them with an excess of confusing price information. The intention is clear – to make price comparisons with rivals impossible in practical terms. The hope is that customers will give up in frustration and stay with or move to well-known companies or brands. Customers signing up for a mobile phone or obtaining a mortgage for house purchase are facing confusion marketing tactics.

Core competencies – the key strengths of an organization (sometimes called 'distinctive capabilities'). Gary Hamel and CK Prahalad, authors of *Competing for the Future*, define core competencies as 'a bundle of skills and technologies (rather than a simple or discrete skill or technology) that enables the company to provide a particular benefit to customers'.

Core competents – the small number of people in an organization who are absolutely vital to that organization's success. Bill Gates has reflected that if 20 people were to leave Microsoft, the company would risk bankruptcy. In a study by the Corporate Leadership Council, a computer firm recognized 100 'core competents' out of 16,000 employees; a software company had 10 out of 11,000; and a transportation group deemed just 20 of its 33,000 as really critical.

Corporate strategy – concerned with mission and vision, portfolio management, acquisitions and divestments. Generic corporate strategies include growth, portfolio extension, caretaking, harvesting or retrenchment.

Cost leadership – when an organization sets out to become the lowest-cost producer in its industry. It does this by exploiting *economies of scale* or *scope* (including marketing and promotional expenditure necessary to maintain reputation or brand image) and the *experience/learning curve* (over time experience results in better ways of doing things and hence lower costs). Cost leadership does *not* imply shoddy goods or poor quality, it simply means delivering goods and services to customers at the quality level expected at the lowest price (as determined by the customer!).

Critical success – factors are the key organizational capabilities that differentiate competitors in the industry in their ability to meet customer needs.

Cultural diagnostics – a vital part of the strategic process because it allows us to become aware of the filters that we use to process our experience, both as individuals and as members of organizations, and the degree of 'selectivity' that is involved in interpreting those experiences. It is a complex area, not least because it deals directly with the foibles that we have as human beings.

Customer intimacy – building customer loyalty in the long term by continually tailoring and shaping products and services to the needs of an increasingly choosy customer. Organizations pursuing this strategy frequently try to build lifetime relationships with their customers.

Customer relationship management (CRM) – a set of techniques and approaches designed to provide personalized service to customers and to increase customer loyalty. Increasingly viewed as a strategic issue, and one that typically requires technological support.

Customer sacrifice – the gap between what customers settle for and what they really want. Successful companies reduce customer sacrifice by cultivating learning relationships. The more customers 'teach' the company, the better it can provide just what they want – and the more difficult it becomes for competitors, to whom customers would have to teach their preferences afresh, to lure them away.

Data mining – the process of using advanced statistical tools to identify commercially useful patterns or relationships in databases.

Data warehouse – a database that can access all of a company's information.

Differentiation – the ability to be unique in the industry along some dimensions valued by the customer. For example, this might be through product or service leadership, or through understanding and knowing customers better than competitors.

Discontinuities – one-off changes in the marketplace that force radical organizational change.

Disintermediation – a buzzword for how the internet is cutting out the middlemen, enabling wholesalers/manufacturers to sell direct to the end user. Classic potential victims of disintermediation are estate agents and travel agents.

Downsizing – restructuring in a declining market where the level of resources (manpower, support functions, etc.) are inappropriate to meeting current customer needs.

e-business – using the internet or other electronic means to conduct business. The two most common models are B2C (Business-to-Consumer) and B2B (Business-to-Business). Partly due to news coverage given to high-profile companies like Amazon, B2C is the better-known model; on the other hand, B2B probably has more long-term potential than its more glamorous cousin.

e-commerce – commercial activity conducted via the internet.

e-lancers – independent contractors connected through personal computers and electronic networks. These electronically connected freelancers – e-lancers – join together into fluid and temporary networks to produce and sell goods and services.

e-tailing – retail strategy based on selling and order processing *via* the web.

External positioning – the relationship of the organization with the external world in terms of its markets, customers and the broader environment.

External risks – dangers posed by the outside world. These might include possible reactions from competitors, and threats to market demand from legislation or substitution.

Five Forces Model – an approach developed by Michael Porter for analysing the competitive environment within which an organization operates. The five forces are the level of rivalry between competitors, threats of substitutes, threats from new entrants, threats from buyers, and threats from sellers.

Focus – a concept popularized by Michael Porter to describe companies that select a market segment or group of segments within an industry and serve customers in these segments to the exclusion of others.

Functional strategies – a tool for translating corporate/business strategies into concrete operational strategies.

Game theory – a branch of mathematical analysis that is increasingly being drawn on by strategists wishing to study decision-making in conflict situations.

Gap analysis – a method for exploring the gap between current reality and the vision of the organization, both in terms of external customer needs and internal capabilities.

Globalization – the integration of economic activity across national or regional boundaries, a process that is being accelerated by the impact of information technology.

Infomediary – a company or individual that makes money by bridging the gap between the need of companies for the capture of detailed customer information and the desire of customers for protection of such information from exploitation by companies.

Informate – a term coined by Harvard academic Shoshana Zuboff to describe the capacity for information technology to translate and make visible organizational processes, objects, behaviours and events.

Innovation – a significant change or improvement in the products or services of an organization or the process by which they are produced.

Intellectual capital – intellectual material – knowledge, information, intellectual property, experience – which can be put to use to create wealth. In a business context, it is the sum total of what employees in an organization know that gives it a competitive edge.

Internal capabilities or **competencies** – what the organization is good at. John Kay refers to distinctive capabilities as 'something an organization can do that its potential competitors cannot … based on its unique set of relationships in the marketplace'.

Internal constraints – factors that can inhibit an organization's ability to achieve desired outcomes. These factors include the level of resources available, knowledge of new markets and products, and the cultural adaptability of the organization to new opportunities.

Intranet – a network designed to organize and share information that is accessible only by a specified group or organization.

Key performance indicators (KPIs) – normally combined as a basket of measures to cover all critical areas of the organization. Although the choice of specific indicators will depend on the unique circumstances of the organization, KPIs are generally selected from the following categories of information: customer satisfaction; product and service innovation; operational improvement; employee morale and commitment; financial health; and cultural diagnosis.

Killer app – a new good or service that, by being first in the market place, dominates it, often returning several hundred per cent on the initial investment.

Knowledge management – a system, most often computer-based, to share information in a company with the goal of increasing levels of responsiveness and innovation.

LOPSOD – Long on Promises, Short on Delivery – a much-hyped product whose performance disappoints.

Mass customization – the cost-efficient mass production as a matter of routine of goods and services in lot sizes of one or just a few at a time.

Meme – an idea, behaviour, or skill that can be transferred from one person to another by imitation. Examples include the way in which we copy ideas, inventions, songs, catch-phrases and stories from one another. In a wired global economy, memes will have the capability of spreading at astonishing speeds.

Mission – many organizations have acknowledged the importance of purpose by framing a formal mission statement. In theory, mission statements should capture the essence of the organization, those things about it that are truly unique and provide the platform from which the organization can create the future. Management writers sometimes refer to this as establishing purpose or strategic intent. The statement takes the form of a formal declaration of what an organization is all about, rooted in a clear understanding of reality. In practical terms, mission statements rarely live up to very much and are often little more than a collection of management buzzwords that are not rooted in organizational reality.

New capitalism – according to Robert Reich, former US Secretary for Labour, 'old capitalism's giant companies had vast numbers of employees; new capitalism's giant companies have few employees. The issues of old capitalism – law on property, contract, limited liability, tort, bankruptcy – all of these are no longer really appropriate. The key assets of new capitalism are not defined as physical property but as intellectual assets, many embedded in people.'

One-to-one marketing – customizing and personalizing a product or service to meet an individual's specific needs.

Operational excellence – providing customers with reliable products or services at competitive prices and delivered with minimal difficulty or inconvenience. The object of the organization adopting this strategy is to lead its industry in price and convenience.

Porter model – this model states that the profitability of an industry is determined by five basic competitive forces:

1 bargaining power of buyers relative to firms in the industry;
2 bargaining power of suppliers relative to firms in the industry;
3 ease of entry of new firms into the industry;
4 availability of substitute products; and
5 intensity of rivalry between existing firms in the industry.

Product leadership – an organization achieves this by creating a continuous stream of state-of-the-art products and services.

Product overlap – occurs when more than one generation of the same product is available simultaneously. The original version of a piece of software may sell at a reduced price alongside the latest version at a higher price.

Prospect theory – according to this theory, people are more motivated by their losses than their gains, and this results in increasingly risky behaviour as losses accumulate. For example, long-odds bets are more popular in the last horse race of the day than the first. By the end of the day, punters have lost most of their gambling money and hope to win it all back with a single long-shot bet that they would not have considered taking in the first race.

Push technology – the delivery of news and multimedia information via the world-wide web to personal computers on people's desks. The web is basically a 'pull' medium. Users decide what they want, point their browsers at the relevant website and then pull the designated pages back to their PCs.

Reality check – any tool, technique, method or device used by individuals or organizations to provide feedback on their place in the world. Reality checks include tools and techniques that are recognized as 'strategic' (such as industry analysis, competitor analysis, and so on) and many others that are not (customer research, employee feedback or merely reading trade magazines). In fact, any exercise to increase organizational awareness is an important part of the strategic process, whether it has a strategic label or not.

Re-purposing – originally coined by US TV executives to describe the process of 'freshening up' a new series of a well-established TV series whose popularity is flagging, by introducing new characters and plot-lines. The term is now being adopted by companies seeking to re-establish forward momentum.

Scenario fixations – believing that one thing is happening when the reality is completely different. In 1988, the warship USS *Vincennes* was involved with potentially hostile Iranian vessels. A series of rapid manoeuvres added to the tension and, in the general confusion, the crew incorrectly identified a civilian Airbus 320 as an Iranian F14 fighter, then misheard its identification signals, and mistakenly thought that it was descending towards the ship when it was in fact on its usual flight path. The warship fired two missiles at the airliner, killing all 290 passengers. The ship's computer system had performed perfectly throughout.

Scenario planning – a tool pioneered by Shell in the 1970s that involves identifying and planning for a range of possible futures. The idea, in a nutshell, is to improve a company's capacity to respond to whichever future comes to pass.

Self-confirming theories – occur when a strategist assumes that what has happened in the past will necessarily be needed in the future.

Seven S model – a widely use analytical tool, devised by Richard Pascale and Anthony Athos, that evaluates organizations under seven key headings to which managers need to pay attention. The seven are: Strategy; Structure; Systems; Skills; Style; Shared values; and Staff. Some of these areas are 'hard' (strategy, structure and systems) and some are 'soft' (style, staff and shared values). 'Skills' is placed centrepiece because it is both 'hard' and 'soft', comprising both the distinctive capabilities of key personnel and the core competencies of the organization as a whole.

Shared vision – in a corporation, a shared vision changes people's relationship with the company. It is no longer 'their company'; it becomes 'our company'. A shared vision is the first step in allowing people who mistrusted each other to begin to work together. It creates a common identity.

Strategic architecture – a term first used by Gary Hamel and CK Prahalad to refer to an organization's high-level blueprint for developing the new competencies and capabilities that it needs to achieve its vision for the future. As such, it emphasizes the importance of the multitude of individual networks and linkages that underlie successful change.

Strategic assets – market position (for example, a monopolistic or oligopolistic position) or relationship with a nation state or regional economic block.

Strategic drift – the financial performance of an organization reflects its key strengths and weaknesses in the past. Incremental changes in key markets may go unnoticed because sales and profits lag behind changes in the reality of the marketplace. The organization may experience its margins and profits being squeezed, yet take comfort in the fact that sales continue to hold up, or even rise. If the organization fails to tackle the root cause of its problems at the customer level, sales will begin to decline and profits may fall precipitously. Strategic drift is often caused when discontinuities go unnoticed because there is a significant time lag before they hit financial performance.

Strategic inflection points – a term coined by Andy Grove to describe a moment in the life of a business when its fundamentals are about to change for better or worse.

Strategic positioning – how an organization can achieve market distinction by performing different activities to those of its rivals, or by performing similar activities in different ways.

SWOT analysis – a tool developed in the 1960s to examine an organization's internal Strengths and Weaknesses as well as the Opportunities and Threats presented by the external competitive environment.

Technology adoption life cycle – a model created by Geoffrey A Moore to demonstrate the various points at which individuals will become involved with a technological innovation. Moore identifies five key groups that will become involved with any new technology at various stages of its life cycle:

1 *Innovators*: the technology enthusiasts;
2 *Early adopters*: the visionaries;
3 *Early majority*: the pragmatists;
4 *Late majority*: the conservatives; and
5 *Laggards*: the sceptics.

Trade-offs – a company must sometime abandon or forgo some product features, services or activities in order to be unique at others. Such trade-offs, in the product and in the value chain, are what make a company truly distinctive. When improvements in the product or in the value chain do not require trade-offs, they often become new best practices that are imitated because competitors can do so with no sacrifice to their existing ways of competing.

Ten X force – a term used by Andy Grove in his book *Only the Paranoid Survive* to describe a super-competitive force that threatens the future of a business.

Unique selling proposition or **USP** – best defined as a company's unique point of difference; the USP of an organization is the unique way in which it matches its internal capabilities with external market opportunities in order to gain competitive advantage.

Value added – in essence, the difference between the value of a firm's output and the cost of the firm's inputs. Technically, it is the difference between the market value of output and the cost of inputs, including the cost of capital (it is the latter which differentiates a value-added statement from a profit or loss statement). It can also be expressed as a ratio (value added as a proportion of a firm's net or gross output). However, in practice measurement of value added is difficult because of the many invisible/psychological attributes of products or services.

Value proposition – a set of benefits that a company can offer its customers, which are different from those that competitors offer.

Viral marketing – releasing a catchy message, typically using online techniques, with a view to the message reaching growing numbers of people, initially organically but then exponentially.

Virtual organization – an organizational form representing a loose combination of technology, expertise and networks.

Vision – a company's view of its future that is compelling and stretching, but also viewed as achievable. A corporate vision for the future has to be grounded in awareness. If not, it quickly becomes a wish-driven strategy – meritorious in all respects except for the fact that it will never be achieved.

ABOUT THE AUTHOR

John Middleton is the founder of the Bristol Management Research Centre. Recognized as a leading expert in personal and systems thinking technologies, he works as a coach and consultant with individuals and organizations who are determined to make best use of the future.

From 1996 to 2001, he published and edited *Future Filter*, a bimonthly business newsletter. He is currently managing editor of *The Friday Filter*, an e-mail-based digest of leading-edge business thinking (www.thefridayfilter.com).

The Ultimate Strategy Library is his seventh book. Previous books include *Writing the New Economy* (Capstone, 2000), and *Smart Things to Know about Your Career* (Capstone, 2001). He also contributed four titles to Capstone's innovative ExpressExec series.

He is working towards a PhD at the University of Bristol.

His e-mail address is: john@thefridayfilter.com

INDEX